Anne Frank House

a museum with a story

Sdu Uitgeverij Koninginnegracht
's-Gravenhage 1992

Anne Frank House

a museum with a story

Anne Frank Stichting
Janrense Boonstra
Marie-José Rijnders

Contents

4

At the end of the 16th century, Amsterdam began a period of great prosperity. There was an enormous increase in trade. Amsterdam became the most important transit port in Europe for grain and wood, among other commodities. Grain was brought in from harbours on the Baltic. Vast amounts of wood came from Norway and were partially used in the shipbuilding industry. Herring fishing and whaling were important, as was trade with Russia. After the establishment of the Dutch East India Company in 1602, trade with the East (i.e. Arabia, China, Japan, India and Persia) greatly expanded. Goods were stored in warehouses and transported further by sea.

The increase in trade and the accelerating growth of the population caused a housing shortage in the city. In 1600 Amsterdam had approximately 50,000 inhabitants. By 1660, this number had grown to about 200,000. In 1610 it was decided to undertake an expansion of Amsterdam. The city development plan was designed and carried out on a grand scale. Round the small inner city a ring of canals was constructed, transected by outwardly radiating streets. Most striking was the spacious design of the three main canals: the Herengracht, the Keizersgracht and the Prinsengracht. The canals and quaysides were much wider than the old ramparts. They were clearly intended to be used as traffic routes for the transport of goods to and from merchants' facilities and warehouses. The space between the canals was also much wider. Now there was room not only for comfortable, deep houses, but also for the construction of gardens – an unknown luxury in the old city.

Every merchant wanted a place on the water. The property along the canals was in great demand and extremely expensive, so narrow, very deep houses were built, affording everyone adequate space on the canal. In order to bring sufficient daylight into these deep structures, they were designed with a 'voorhuis' (literally a 'front house') and an 'achterhuis' ('back house' or 'back annexe') connected to each other by a hall. The interior space which was thus created between the front house and the back annexe allowed daylight to enter even the back rooms of the front house. The back

Amsterdam city map after 1610. The canal pattern is clearly recognizable. The western part of the city is already fully built up.

annexe usually had windows along the rear wall looking out onto the enclosed garden. The depth of a front house could run from twelve to fifteen metres; a back annexe could vary from four to nine metres. The connecting hall was of a similar length. In this way, a canalside house could be as deep as 30 metres.

In order to bring goods in and out of the building, all buildings were supplied with a hoisting hook. Most of the canalside houses were used as residences and warehouses. The house at 263 Prinsengracht, which would later be known as the Anne Frank House, was built along with its neighbour, no. 265, by Dirk van Delft in 1635. In 1739 the house was restored: a new front façade was built, and the small back annexe was taken down and replaced by a higher one. Over the years the building was used as a warehouse and as a private residence. In 1841 the ground floor served for a short time as a stable for five horses. At the beginning of this century, a firm which manufactured stoves, heaters, and beds took up residence there. Around 1930 the house came to be used as a workshop for the production of piano rolls. By 1939 the house stood empty.

The Frank family

Anne Frank, through whom the house at 263 Prinsengracht later would be known the world over, originally came from Germany. She was born on 12 June 1929, in Frankfurt am Main, the second daughter of Otto Frank and Edith Frank-Holländer. Her sister Margot was three years older. Otto Frank's mother belonged to a Jewish family that had lived in Frankfurt for hundreds of years. He was born in 1889, the same year in which Adolf Hitler came into the world in Braunau, Austria. Otto's father was owner and director of a banking firm, and it was assumed that his son would follow in his footsteps. But matters progressed quite differently as a consequence of the First World War, which raged in Europe from 1914 to 1918. Otto Frank served in the German army and fought at the front in France. He rose to the rank of lieutenant. The family business suffered great losses during the war. In an attempt to pump new life into the

The Prinsengracht at the end of the thirties.

Westerkerk and surroundings around 1950. The Annexe is visible in the middle of the photo.

business, it was decided to go international. In 1923 Otto Frank went to Amsterdam to set up a Dutch branch of the 'Bank M. Frank & Zonen'. The undertaking met with negligible success and went into liquidation after one year. During this period he came to know Mr Kleiman, who later would play an important role when the family went into hiding in the Secret Annexe. Back in Frankfurt, Otto Frank married Edith Holländer in the spring of 1925. She came from Aachen and was eleven years younger than Otto. On 16 February 1926 Margot was born. Otto had resumed working in Frankfurt, trying with his brother Herbert to save the family business. But the unfavourable situation in post-war Germany was exacerbated by the economic crisis of 1929. The business activities of the bank continued to decline.

The Nazis come to power

The crisis in Germany at the end of the 1920s played right into the hands of a still-unknown party in Munich. The National Socialist German Workers Party, abbreviated as the NSDAP, was set up there in 1920. Its adherents were called 'Nazis'. Adolf Hitler, a member from the beginning, quickly managed to work his way up to leader ('Führer'). In Munich he made an abortive attempt at a coup for which he received a short prison sentence. While in prison, he put his ideas into words in a book entitled *Mein Kampf* (*My Struggle*). When Hitler later came to power, this book became the standard work of Nazi Germany. In his book Hitler lashed out against the Jews, the most inferior 'race' in his eyes. In doing so he was taking up the claims of anti-Semitism, which had existed for centuries and at the end of the 19th century had assumed a racist character. The superiority of the 'Aryan' race was proclaimed at that time in pseudo-scientific theories. This Aryan, or Germanic, race, to which all Germans belonged, was the strongest and the best: all other races were of lesser value. Hitler blamed the Jews for everything that had gone wrong in Germany in recent years: the German defeat in the First World War, the economic and financial crisis and the widespread unemployment.

Otto and Edith Frank on their honeymoon in Italy, spring 1925.

Otto Frank with
Margot and Anne on
his lap, 1931.

Edith Frank with her two daughters in
Frankfurt, March 1933.

Pages 12–13:
Berlin, 1 May 1938.
Hitler addressing a
mass rally.

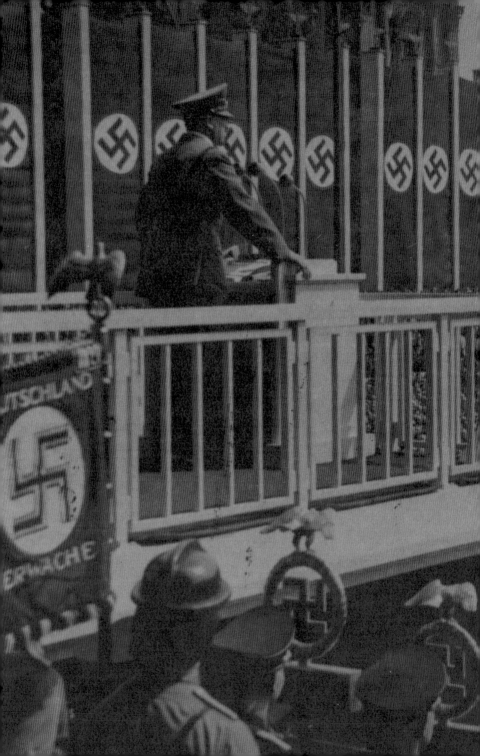

He made a scapegoat of the Jews, making them easy prey to many in Germany. The influence of the National Socialists increased. The NSDAP grew from a small party to a mass movement which could no longer be ignored by the established political parties. In the 1932 elections the NSDAP took around 37% of the votes. This success, plus great dissension within the other parties, resulted in the NSDAP forming a new government. On 30 January 1933, Hitler was named chancellor. Within a few years he managed to assume total power. Germany was no longer a democracy but a dictatorship and would remain so until 1945.

The Frank family moves to Amsterdam

The growing number of Nazi adherents in the early '30s caused Otto Frank great concern, not only for his business activities but also for the future of his children. It had long been clear that no prospects existed for Jews now that Hitler had come to power. Only two months after Hitler's appointment, municipal elections were held in Germany. In spite of its terroristic approach, the NSDAP managed to win only 44% of the votes. In Frankfurt the newly-elected Jewish mayor was discharged and the first anti-Jewish regulations were quickly put into operation. The party army, known as the SA ('Sturmabteilung'), enthusiastically lent its strength to carrying out these regulations. For Otto Frank, all this meant that the declining family business had no chance of success. A general boycott of Jewish shops and businesses on 1 April 1933 deepened the hopelessness of the situation. Despite the poor showing of the Amsterdam branch of the family bank, Otto Frank had good memories of the Netherlands. The plan to emigrate to the Netherlands because of developments in Germany began to take more definite shape. In the summer of 1933 the opportunity arose to set up a commercial branch of the Opekta firm. Opekta manufactured pectin, a substance which in powder form was frequently used at that time in preparing homemade jam.

A Jewish-owned shop in Frankfurt covered with anti-Semitic slogans, 1933.

During the night of November 9-10, 1938, synagogues and Jewish shops were destroyed throughout Germany. This is the Munich synagogue after this so-called 'Kristallnacht'.

A few years before, Otto Frank's brother-in-law similarly had set up a branch office in Switzerland. Otto Frank decided to leave Frankfurt with his family. His wife and daughters remained behind with his mother-in-law in Aachen while he continued on to Amsterdam to set up the branch office and to find suitable housing for himself and his family. He found a home on the Merwedeplein, which was situated in the newly-built southern part of the city. Edith Frank and Margot moved to Amsterdam in the beginning of December 1933. Anne came from Aachen to Amsterdam in February 1934, where she *'was put on Margot's table as a birthday present'*, as she later wrote in her diary on 20 June 1942.

The first years in the Netherlands

While the consequences of Nazi politics were making themselves ever more evident in Germany a year after the take-over, relative calm reigned in the Netherlands. The First World War had passed over the neutral Netherlands entirely. For the Frank family and around twenty thousand other Jews who had succeeded in getting out of Germany and coming to the Netherlands, it seemed a safe haven of refuge. For Margot and Anne, there was apparently nothing standing in the way of a carefree childhood. They both quickly learned to speak Dutch and found new friends to play with in their new surroundings. There were other Jewish immigrants from Germany living round the Merwedeplein with whom the Franks had contact. Sundays were often a day for visits. The dentist Friedrich Pfeffer, who later would go into hiding with them (Anne renamed him 'Dussel' in her diary) belonged to this circle of acquaintances. During those years Anne attended the Montessori kindergarten and primary school in the Niersstraat, now called the Anne Frank School. The façade is brightly painted with a quotation from Anne's diary.

There was steady improvement for Otto Frank's branch of Opekta during this period. Begun as a one-man business, Otto had taken on several staff members over

An ordinary shop in Germany in the thirties. Under the small swastika and the text 'German merchant' are the words 'Jews not welcome!'

Anne and her girlfriend Sanne Ledermann, Merwedeplein 1935.

Margot in the neigh-
bourhood of
the Merwedeplein.

the course of time. Among them were Victor Kugler, his right-hand man, whom Anne called 'Kraler' in her diary, and Hermine ('Miep') Santrouschitz. Miep would later be one of the most important helpers when the family was in hiding. In 1934 the business moved from the Nieuwe Zijds Voorburgwal to a building on the Singel. The product manufactured by Opekta was seasonal. Sales were limited to summertime and immediately afterward, when fruit was available to be made into jam. For this reason Otto Frank looked for a second, less seasonal product. He found it in the form of an herb mixture used in the production of sausages, and a new business was set up in 1938 under the name 'Pectacon'. Hermann van Pels, a Jewish immigrant returning from Germany, was taken on as specialist for this product. With his wife and small son Peter he had fled from Osnabrück a year earlier to escape the Nazis. Van Pels and his family would later be the second family to take cover in the Secret Annexe. Anne called them 'the Van Daan family' in her diary, the name which will also be used here. The previously mentioned Kleiman, whom Otto had met in 1924, became the bookkeeper for both businesses. Anne called him 'Koophuis' in her diary. One last person who should be mentioned here is Bep Voskuijl, who came in 1937 to assist Miep. She also reappears in Anne's diary but under the name 'Elly'.

Otto Frank's entry card for the Rotterdam stock exchange, September 1933. Position no. 80 was for 'Opekta'.

Opekta advertising poster; the same one hangs on the wall of Anne's room.

Anne, second from left, on her tenth birthday in front of the house on the Merwedeplein.

Miep Santrouschitz
and Otto Frank in the
Opekta office on the
Singel, before 1940.

The war years

On 10 May 1940, German troops invaded the Netherlands. The struggle lasted only a few days. After the heavy bombardment of Rotterdam, with the threat of repeated attacks on other cities, the Netherlands surrendered. Five years of occupation followed, bringing to an end the tranquillity and safety which the Jewish refugees from Germany had sought. A few were able to escape at the last moment and flee abroad, to England, for example. Several hundred people took their own lives during those days in May. The population waited to see what the occupation would mean for the Netherlands, but they hoped that the situation would be better than it had been in Germany.

During the first months there was relatively little change on the face of things. Applying a moderate political approach, the occupiers tried to win the Dutch over. According to Nazi beliefs, the Netherlands was inhabited by a fraternal – Germanic – people who would fit perfectly in the Great German Reich. Naturally, for the approximately one hundred and forty thousand Jews in the Netherlands a 'solution' would have to be found. After the summer of 1940, the solution was clear: the practice of isolating Jewish men, women and children from the rest of the population would be taken up in the Netherlands as well. This process went into operation almost unnoticed with the introduction of the so-called Aryan Declaration. All Dutch civil servants had to affirm their 'Aryan' or 'non-Aryan' origins by signing a declaration. The first division between Jew and non-Jew thus became a fact. In November 1940 all Jewish civil servants were dismissed.

263 Prinsengracht

On 1 December 1940, about a half year after the German invasion, Otto Frank moved the Opekta and Pectacon offices and warehouses from 400 Singel to 263 Prinsengracht. On the ground floor of this building was a large storage space consisting of three sections. The front section became dispatch office. The machines for grinding

Entry of the Germans into Amsterdam. A small group of people give the Hitler salute.

De ondergeteekende,

beroep
betrekking ,

geboren den   te ,

wonende te ,

verklaart, dat naar $\frac{zijn}{haar}$ beste weten noch $\frac{hijzelf}{zijzelf}$, noch $\frac{zijn}{haar}$ $\frac{echtgenoot(e)}{verloofde}$ *), noch een $\frac{zijner\ (harer)}{hunner}$ ouders of grootouders ooit heeft behoord tot de Joodsche geloofsgemeenschap.

Aan de(n) ondergeteekende is bekend, dat $\frac{hij}{zij}$ zich, ingeval vorenstaande verklaring niet juist blijkt te zijn, aan onmiddellijk ontslag blootstelt.

, 1940.

(handteekening)

*) Doorschrappen ingeval de ambtenaar niet gehuwd of verloofd is.

Ⓐ 5936 - '40

The Aryan Declaration, which all Dutch civil servants were required to fill in. False information meant immediate dismissal.

Anne and Margot on the beach at Zandvoort, August 1940.

and mixing spices were located in the middle, and in the back the spices were packed. The building had four entrance doors. The double warehouse doors were on the right side. To the left of these was the door giving access to the offices on the first floor. The front door on the extreme left opened to a steep stairway which led to former living accommodation on the second floor. Here there were three rooms. On the street side were mixing tubs for the Opekta firm in which the gelling substance used in jam preparation was made. In the middle room the basic ingredients lay stored in stacks. The spices were stacked up in the back room. The attic on the third floor of the front house was used for storage. A narrow stairway led to a loft. The first floor of the back annexe formerly had been one large room. When Opekta took over the building, a wall was built to create two rooms: Otto Frank's office to the left and the office kitchen to the right. The third floor of the back annexe was used as a laboratory for a short time.

The persecution of the Jews begins

While Otto Frank's business had changed addresses three times, the family continued to live on the Merwedeplein. Anne was in the highest class at the Montessori primary school. The regulation restricting Jewish children to Jewish schools, which had been enforced in Germany since 1938, was also put into effect in the Netherlands. In September 1941 Anne went to the Jewish Secondary School, as did Margot who was a few years ahead.

There were many more changes in store for the Dutch Jews in 1941. The true nature of the occupiers was becoming more and more evident. All Dutch citizens had been registered according to religion. The identity cards of Jews were now stamped with a black letter 'J'. Freedom of movement was restricted for Jews: they were no longer permitted to
ride the trams or to drive cars. Jews could shop only during certain hours and in certain stores. They were not allowed into theatres, cinemas or restaurants. Everywhere there appeared signs with texts such as 'No Jews allowed' or 'Forbidden for Jews'. Jews

The entrance in 1942.

Warehouse and workplace on the ground floor.

May 1941, in the front office: from left to right, Esther (an office worker), Bep Voskuijl, Van Daan and Miep Santrouschitz.

were also required to wear the Jewish star in public. Anne would later write in her diary: *'So we could not do this and were forbidden to do that. But life went on in spite of it all. Jacque [ed.: a girl-friend] used to say to me, "You're scared to do anything, because it may be forbidden." '*

In the last week of February 1941 the first round-ups and arrests took place. Four hundred Jewish men were picked up on the Waterlooplein in Amsterdam. This would be the first group in the Netherlands to be deported to a concentration camp. Only two of these four hundred men survived the war. In protest against this round-up, a strike broke out in Amsterdam and the surrounding area which is still commemorated in the Netherlands every year on 25 February.

In the course of 1941 it became clear to Otto Frank that he could no longer keep the business under his own name. Sooner or later, the occupiers would forbid Jews to own their own business in the Netherlands as well. In Germany, Jewish businesses had already been closed and taken over by the Nazis, who then appointed a 'Verwalter', a deputy, to carry on the business under their authority. In order to avoid this, Otto stepped down as director of Pectacon on 4 April 1941, and appointed Kleiman in his place. A month later, the name 'Pectacon' was changed to 'Gies & Co.' The name Gies was borrowed from Jan Gies, Miep's fiancé. He was also a friend of the Frank family and helped Otto with his affairs. In December of that year Otto withdrew from the directorship of Opekta as well. This firm was also able to continue under the official leadership of Mr Kleiman.

The hiding place is made ready

Although the business appeared to be secure, Otto Frank continued to worry about the future. Until 1940 he had taken it for granted that his home in the Netherlands was safe. Even when the Netherlands became occupied, he hoped at first that the persecution of the Jews in the Netherlands would not run to such extremes. Many shared

Jews wearing the compulsory star on the streets of Amsterdam. A small group of Germans in the background.

16 July 1941:
Otto Frank and Anne
at the wedding of
Miep and Jan Gies.

Mr and Mrs van Daan (left) and Mr Kugler.

Miep and Jan Gies at
their wedding.

his hope, but events proved otherwise. In January 1942, Otto Frank was obliged to file a request for emigration, a procedure required of all non-Dutch Jews. In this way the Germans hoped to find out precisely which Jews were not yet listed in their files. On the Frank family's application receipt the first names are changed. German Jews had been required since 1939 to add the names 'Israel' or 'Sara' to their first names. The actual first names were omitted from the Frank's receipt, however, either by mistake or on purpose.

Then the idea arose of turning the back annexe on the Prinsengracht into a 'hiding place' ('onderduikplaats'). The Dutch word 'onderduiken', literally 'to dive under' or 'to submerge', came into existence during the war. Whenever people chose to hide from the occupiers (to escape the threat of deportation to Germany, for example), this was called 'onderduiken'. In many cases, people 'dived under' on farms or in forests in the countryside. Otto Frank chose a less obvious place: the back annexe of his own office building.

During the first months of 1942, furniture, household goods and provisions were moved into the back annexe as unobtrusively as possible. The attic area and the two floors beneath it were cleared and made somewhat liveable. Only Otto's closest co-workers, Kleiman, Kugler and Miep Gies, were aware of the preparations taking place. Bep, the assistant, had not yet become involved. Her father was employed at that time as warehouse manager on the ground floor. Neither he nor the two warehouse employees had been made aware of the plan. Everything took place in the deepest secrecy.

Despite this high level of preparedness, the immediate reason for going into hiding came as a startling surprise. On Sunday, 5 July 1942, a call-up from the German Sicherheitsdienst (Security Service) was delivered on the Merwedeplein, addressed to Margot. The following day she was to report for transport to a 'workcamp' in Germany. A thousand other Jewish boys and girls (Margot was just sixteen at the time) received the same call-up that day. Otto Frank decided that their decision to go into hiding

Anne in the first class at the Jewish Secondary School, 1941.

The Frank family in the Merwedeplein, 1941.

Margot, around 1941.

could be delayed no longer, and on Monday morning, July 6, the Frank family moved into the back annexe. Events in the 'Secret Annexe', as it came it be called, are elaborately described by Anne in the diary which she had received as a gift for her thirteenth birthday a few weeks earlier.

In hiding

On 9 July 1942, Anne gave a detailed description of the building in her diary: *'I will describe the building: there is a large warehouse on the ground floor which is used as a store and is subdivided into various little compartments, such as the milling room, where cinnamon, clove and substitute pepper are ground up, and the stockroom. The front door to the house is next to the warehouse door, and inside the front door is a second doorway which leads to a staircase. There is another door at the top of the stairs with a frosted glass window in it, which has "Office" written in black letters across it. This is the large main office, very big, very light, and very full. Bep,*

Miep and Mr Kleiman work there in the daytime. A small dark room containing the safe, a wardrobe and a large cupboard, leads to a small, stuffy, somewhat dark second office. Mr Kugler and Mr van Daan used to sit here, now it is only Mr Kugler. One can reach Kugler's office from the passage, but only via a glass door which can be opened from the inside but not from the outside. From Kugler's office a long passage goes past the coal store, up four steps and leads to the show-room of the whole building, the private office. Dark, dignified furniture, linoleum and carpets on the floor, radio, smart lamp, everything first-class. Next door there is a roomy kitchen with a hot-water faucet and a gas stove and next door the w.c. That is the first floor.

'A wooden staircase leads from the downstairs passage to the next floor. There is a small landing at the top. There is a door to the right and left of the landing, the left one leading to the front of the house, with spice room, corridor room, a front room, and to the attics. One of those really steep Dutch staircases runs from the side to the other door opening on to the street.

'To the right of the landing lies our "Secret Annexe." No one would ever guess that there would be so many rooms hidden behind that plain gray door. There's a little step in front of the

Receipt for the
emigration request
which Otto Frank
filed in January
1942.

Name:
Naam:

Vorname:
Voornaam:

Antrag überreicht am:
Aanvraag afgegeven op:

Zentralstelle für jüdische
Auswanderung Amsterdam
Adama v. Scheltemaplein 1
Telefoon 97001

N⁰ 136094

OPROEPING!

Aan   Vorst-de Vries Lea,15-7-88   L   No.
Deurloostreat 99'

U moet zich voor eventueele deelname aan een, onder politietoezichtstaande, werk-
verruiming in Duitschland voor persoonsonderzoek en geneeskundige keuring naar het door-
gangskamp Westerbork, station Hooghalen, begeven.

Daartoe moet U op .... om .... uur

op de verzamelplaats .... aanwezig zijn

Als bagage mag medegenomen worden:

  1 koffer of rugzak
  1 paar werklaarzen
  2 paar sokken
  2 onderbroeken
  2 hemden
  1 werkpak
  2 wollen dekens
  2 stel beddengoed (overtrek met laken)
  1 eetnap
  1 drinkbeker
  1 lepel en
  1 pullover
  handdoek en toiletartikelen

en eveneens marschproviand voor 3 dagen en alle aan U uitgereikte distributiekaarten met
inbegrip van de distributiestamkaart.
De mee te nemen bagage moet in gedeelten gepakt worden.

a.   **Noodzakelijke reisbehoeften**
daartoe behooren: 2 dekens, 1 stel beddegoed, levensmiddelen voor 3 dagen, toiletgerei,
etensbord, eetbestek, drinkbeker,

b.   **Groote bagage**
De onder b. vermelde bagage moet worden gepakt in een stevige koffer of rugzak,
welke op duidelijke wijze voorzien moet zijn van **naam, voornamen, geboortedatum
en het woord „Holland".**
Gezinsbagage is niet toegestaan.
Het voorgaande moet nauwkeurig in acht genomen worden, daar de groote bagage in
de plaats van vertrek afzonderlijk ingeladen wordt.
De verschillende bewijs- en persoonspapieren en 'distributiekaarten met inbegrip van
de distributiestamkaart mogen **niet bij de bagage verpakt worden,** doch moeten,
voor onmiddellijk vertoon gereed, medegedragen worden.
De woning moet ordelijk achtergelaten en afgesloten worden, de huissleutels moeten
worden medegenomen.
Niet medegenomen mogen worden: levend huisraad.

K 372

The war years

A call-up for a workcamp in Germany such as the one Margot received on 5 July 1942.
Everything which may be brought along is carefully listed.

door and then you are inside. There is a steep staircase immediately opposite the entrance. On the left a tiny passage brings you into a room, this room was to become the Frank family's bed-sitting-room, next door an even smaller room, study and bedroom for the two young ladies of the family. On the right a little room without windows, containing the washbasin and small w.c. compart-ment, with another door leading to Margot's and my room. If you go up the next flight of stairs and open the door, you are simply amazed that there could be such a big light room in such an old house by the canal. There is a stove in this room (thanks to the fact that it was used before as Kugler's laboratory) and a sink. This is now the kitchen as well as bedroom for the Van Daan couple, besides being general living room, dining room and scullery. A tiny little corridor room will become Peter van Daan's apartment. Then just as on the lower landing there is a large attic. So there you are, I have introduced you to the whole of our beautiful "Secret Annexe!"'

A week after the arrival of the Frank family, business partner Van Daan and his family also went into hiding in the Secret Annexe. They moved into the uppermost floor. '*The Van Daans arrived on July 13. We thought they were coming on the fourteenth, but between the thirteenth and sixteenth of July the Germans called up people right and left which created more and more unrest, so they played for safety, better a day too early than a day too late. At nine-thirty in the morning (we were still having breakfast) Peter arrived, the Van Daan's son, not sixteen yet, a rather, soft, shy, gawky youth; can't expect much from his company. Mr and Mrs Van Daan arrived half an hour later.*' (14 August 1942).

A few months later, on 16 November 1942, the eighth and last person to join the company in hiding finally arrived. From that time onwards Anne had to share her little room with the dentist Pfeffer. She called him 'Dussel' in her diary, the name which also will be used here.

It can be concluded from Anne's descriptions that the Secret Annexe was not lux-urious. It was not possible to manage a thorough redecoration of rooms used for hiding. The rooms had dark green panelling. The old, yellowed wallpaper hung loose in places and revealed damp spots and streaks of leakage. In the 'Prospectus and

The kitchen on the first floor of the Annexe.

The wall of Anne's room with photos and movie star collection.
The Opekta poster is to the right.

Stairway from the first floor
to the landing in front of the
Annexe entrance.
The windows are covered
over with opaque paper.

The 'growth marks' on a wall in the Frank family's bedroom. The children's growth was monitored in this way.

'One of those really steep Dutch staircases' going to the second floor of the front house.

The small window-less room that served as a washing room.

The attic of the Annexe.

Guide to the "Secret Annexe" ', written by Van Daan on the occasion of Dussel's arrival, there is also mention of '*running water in the bathroom (alas, no bath) and down various inside and outside walls*'.

Daily life

The eight in hiding tried as much as possible to lead a 'normal' life. To begin with, this meant regularity: rising, eating, working, resting and the like according to schedule. This regularity was also forced upon them by circumstances to a great extent. The inhabitants of the Annexe had to take into account the working hours of the people in the office and in the warehouse. In such an old canalside house with its wooden floors, each sound easily penetrated downwards. On the ground floor, people were working who must know nothing about those in hiding. Occasionally there would be visitors in the office, and the neighboring building was also a place of work. So those in hiding had to keep as still as possible between eight-thirty in the morning and five-thirty in the evening. This was the case six days a week, for the office was open on Saturday morning as well. Fortunately, the long day was interrupted by a lunch break. The warehouse employees then went home to eat.

The helpers of the eight in hiding usually visited the Secret Annexe during the lunch break. Anne wrote about this on 5 August 1943: '*Quarter to one. The place is filling up. First Mr Gies, then Kleiman or Kugler, Bep and sometimes Miep as well. One o'clock. We're all sitting listening to the BBC seated around the little baby radio; these are the sole times when the members of the "Secret Annexe" do not interrupt each other, because here someone is speaking even Mr Van Daan can't interrupt. Quarter past one. The great share-out. Everyone from below gets a cup of soup, and if there is ever a pudding some of that as well. Mr Gies is happy and goes to sit on the divan or lean against the writing table. Newspaper, cup and usually cat, beside him. If one of the three is missing, he is sure to protest. Kleiman tells us the latest news from town; he is certainly an excellent source of information. Kugler comes helter-skelter upstairs – a short, firm*

Left, Peter van Daan.
Right, Mr Dussel.

The old draining-board in the communal kitchen used by the Annexe inhabitants.

knock on the door and in he comes rubbing his hands, according to his mood in a good temper and talkative or bad-tempered and quiet. Quarter to two. Everyone rises from the table and goes about his own business. Margot and Mummy to the dishes, Mr and Mrs Van Daan to the divan, Peter up to the attic, Daddy to the divan, Dussel to his bed and Anne to her work.'

For the inhabitants of the Secret Annexe, Sunday was always a day full of activity: '*What other people do during the week, the people in the Secret Annexe do on Sunday. When other people put on nice clothes and go for a walk in the sun, we stay here, scrubbing, sweeping and washing,*' Anne wrote on 20 February 1944. The wash was done in the office kitchen on the first floor, where there was a hot-water heater. Due to the growing absence of soap and soap powder, the job of washing and scrubbing became an increasingly heavy chore. Anne wrote that compared with other Jews who did not choose to go under cover, those in hiding in the Secret Annexe were actually living in a paradise, but they did sense that they had 'sunk': '*By this I mean that our manners have declined. For instance, ever since we have been here we have had one oilcloth on our table which, owing to so much use, is not one of the cleanest. Admittedly I often try to clean it with a dirty dishcloth, which is more hole than cloth and which was new before we went into hiding long ago. The table doesn't do us much credit either, in spite of hard scrubbing. The Van Daans have been sleeping on the same flannelette sheet the whole winter. One can't wash it here because the soap powder we get on the ration isn't sufficient, and besides it's not good enough. Daddy goes about in frayed trousers and his tie is beginning to show signs of wear too.*' (2 May 1943)

Rubbish was, as much as possible, burned in the heaters in the Annexe. This took place after office hours and early Sunday morning. Summers were no exception: '*Although it is obviously warm we have to light our fires every other day, in order to burn vegetable peelings and refuse. We can't put anything in the garbage pails, because we must always think of the warehouseman. How easily one could be betrayed by being a little careless!*' Anne wrote on 18 May 1943.

The space in the Annexe, filled with tables, chairs, cabinets and beds, was often rather cramped for its eight inhabitants. In the evenings and on Sunday, they could

The window in Anne's room.
In this post-war photo the remains of the old curtains are still visible.

The back façade of the Annexe. The window with the half-curtain is that in Anne's room.

make use of the other areas of the building. Thus Mr Dussel often studied during the evening in Otto Frank's private office. Peter went to the warehouse each evening to feed the cat or to empty the ash bin from the heater into the office garbage pail. Anne often took the occasion to go to the front of the office and peek out. After a couple of break-ins occurred in the office and warehouse areas, these 'outings' in the building were forbidden. The longer the time in hiding went on, the greater the irritation among the inhabitants grew.

For Anne, Margot and Peter, daily life meant homework and lessons so that they wouldn't fall too far behind in school. Otto Frank continued the lessons from the Jewish Secondary School with help from some school books he'd brought along. Under Bep's name, Margot signed up for a correspondence course in Latin and, together with Anne, took up a course in stenography. Miep regularly went to the library to borrow books under her own name for the group in hiding.

Anne spent more and more of her free time with her writing. When the first diary was full she continued to write in other notebooks, on loose copy pages and even in an accounts book. Margot also kept a diary but it has been lost.

The Annexe as hiding place

From the block of buildings that ran along the garden side behind the Prinsengracht during the war years, the back annexe of no. 263 was but one in a long row. There were large and small buildings, and some houses were deeper than others. At a number of places additions had been built far into the garden, among them 265 Prinsengracht next to Otto Frank's office building. The neighbours who lived next door and behind were under the impression that the back annexe was not in use. It was known that this was part of the office building because Miep occasionally left the windows open to bring in fresh air.

When the time in hiding began, rules had to be laid down to prevent anyone from

The door to the front house opposite the bookcase. A wooden plate was fastened over the pane.

The entrance to the Annexe.

seeing inside. Anne wrote on 11 July 1942: '*We are very nervous in other ways, too, that the neighbours might hear us or see something going on. We made curtains straight away on the first day. Really one can hardly call them curtains, they are just light, loose strips of material, all different shapes, quality, and pattern, which Daddy and I sewed together in a most unprofessional way. These works of art are fixed in position with drawing pins, not to come down until we emerge from here.*' As soon as it was dark, the inhabitants placed blackout partitions in front of the windows. Only then could the lights go on. Few who lived in the surrounding area could suspect that the back part of the building was being used as a hiding place. The Secret Annexe had to be camouflaged inside as well. For this purpose, Bep's father, Mr Voskuijl, who had been told about the people in hiding, built the swinging book case in August 1942. This was placed in front of the entrance door on the landing so that it looked as though the house stopped there. A wooden plate was fastened over the pane in the door leading from the landing to the front house.

The back annexe was withdrawn from view in other ways as well. The windows in the landing were pasted over with opaque paper. The windows along the back of the front house were painted blue. This was done under the pretext that sunlight was harmful to the herbs that were stored here. Everything possible was done to prevent warehouse personnel from crossing the landing to the back annexe. They were left with the illusion that the former laboratory was empty. Despite all this, it was difficult to keep the back annexe hidden. After the war, Kugler said that he caught the new warehouse manager, Voskuijl's successor, scratching away the blue paint on the window of the second floor front house and saying, '*Well, well, I've never been over there.*'

The helpers

When the group first went into hiding, four of Otto Frank's co-workers were told of the situation. First, of course, was Kleiman, who had taken Otto Frank's place as official director of both businesses. Victor Kugler, Miep Gies and the typist Bep Voskuijl were

The 'Jewish' star, compulsory after April 1942.

VLEESCH	VLEESCH	VLEESCH	VLEESCH	VLEESCH	VLEESCH	VLEESCH	VLEESCH
48 A	47 A	46 A	45 A	44 A	43 A	42 A	41 A
48 B	47 B	46 B	45 B	44 B	43 B	42 B	41 B
VLEESCH	VLEESCH	VLEESCH	VLEESCH	VLEESCH	VLEESCH	VLEESCH	VLEESCH

VOEDINGSMIDDELEN VOOR HOUDERS VAN INLEGVELLEN GA 401
11e EN 12e PERIODE 1944 (1 OCTOBER–25 NOVEMBER) | BONKAART KA 411-412 | LAND

RESERVE	RESERVE	RESERVE	RESERVE	RESERVE	RESERVE	RESERVE	RESERVE
A 95	A 93	A 91	A 89	A 87	A 85	A 83	A 81
RESERVE	RESERVE	RESERVE	RESERVE	RESERVE	RESERVE	RESERVE	RESERVE
A 96	A 94	A 92	A 90	A 88	A 86	A 84	A 82

BROOD	BROOD	BROOD	BROOD	BROOD	BROOD	BROOD	BROOD
48 A (4)	47 A (4)	46 A (4)	45 A (4)	44 A (4)	43 A (4)	42 A (4)	41 A (4)
48 A (3)	47 A (3)	46 A (3)	45 A (3)	44 A (3)	43 A (3)	42 A (3)	41 A (3)
48 A (2)	47 A (2)	46 A (2)	45 A (2)	44 A (2)	43 A (2)	42 A (2)	41 A (2)
48 A (1)	47 A (1)	46 A (1)	45 A (1)	44 A (1)	43 A (1)	42 A (1)	41 A (1)
48 B	47 B	46 B	45 B	44 B	43 B	42 B	41 B
48 B	47 B	46 B	45 B	44 B	43 B	42 B	41 B
BROOD	BROOD	BROOD	BROOD	BROOD	BROOD	BROOD	BROOD

Ration cards, needed for buying food.

A shopping list for the butcher that Van Daan made for Miep Gies.

also drawn in. Miep's husband Jan was in on the plan as well. Both Miep and Jan made a late-night visit to the Merwedeplein on the night before the Franks went into hiding. They were the last visitors at this address. '*At eleven o'clock Miep and Jan Gies arrived. Miep has been in the business with Daddy since 1933 and has become a close friend, likewise her brand-new husband, Jan. Once again, shoes, stockings, books and underclothes disappeared into Miep's bag and Jan's deep pockets; and at eleven-thirty they too disappeared,*' Anne wrote a few days later.

After 6 July 1942, the fate of the inhabitants of the Secret Annexe lay totally in the hands of the helpers. They knew how great the risks were. There were severe penalties for those who helped people go into hiding: the threat that a helper could also be sent to a camp loomed very large. The four helpers from the office took care of food, clothing, medicine, books and whatever else was needed. Many products were difficult to obtain and more and more were becoming unavailable. The basic necessities of life were being rationed. Food could be bought only with official ration cards. For the inhabitants of the Secret Annexe, who were living an illegal life, there were no ration cards. The helpers had to go to all possible lengths to find food. Through the resistance, it was possible to obtain stolen or counterfeit ration cards which could not be distinguished from real ones. Sometimes cards could be bought on the black market where the prices, of course, were shockingly high.

Help also came from the outside, although these outsiders did not know the whereabouts of those in hiding. Van Daan had earlier introduced Miep to a friendly butcher through whom she often was able to buy meat without a ration card. The eight in hiding needed a considerable amount of bread every day. Mr Kleiman had dealings with a baker who delivered bread without the required ration card. The baker notated the number of cards owed to him. When Kleiman returned from prison, he looked up the baker in order to pay his debt. It appeared that he owed 400 bread cards. One bread card at that time cost 40 guilders on the black market. When Kleiman said with

alarm that he didn't have that much money, the baker simply crossed out his bill without saying a word.

On Monday, 3 April 1944, Anne wrote: '*Contrary to my usual custom, I will for once write more fully about food because it has become a very difficult and important matter, not only here in the "Secret Annexe" but in the whole of Holland, all Europe, and even beyond. In the twenty-one months that we've spent here we have been through a good many "food cycles" – you'll understand what that means in a minute. When I talk of "food cycles" I mean periods in which one has nothing else to eat but one particular dish or kind of vegetable. We had nothing but endive for a long time, day in, day out, endive with sand, endive without sand, stew with endive, boiled or en casserole; then it was spinach, and after that followed kohlrabi, salsify, cucumbers, tomatoes, sauerkraut, etc., etc. For instance, it's really disagreeable to eat a lot of sauerkraut for lunch and supper every day, but you do it if you're hungry. However, we have the most delightful period of all now, because we don't get any greens at all. Our weekly menu for supper consists of kidney beans, pea soup, potatoes with dumplings, potato-cholent and, by the grace of God, occasionally turnip tops or rotten carrots, and then the kidney beans once again. We eat potatoes at every meal, beginning with breakfast, because of the bread shortage, but they are still a bit warm then. We make our soup from kidney or haricot beans, potatoes, Julienne soup in packets, thick chicken soup in packets, kidney beans in packets. Everything contains beans, not to mention the bread! In the evening we always have potatoes with gravy substitute and – thank goodness we've still got it – beetroot salad.*'

The problem of providing daily food for the inhabitants of the Secret Annexe became greater as the occupation continued and goods became more scarce. Accompanying this was the constant pressure under which the helpers and inhabitants lived: the fear of being discovered or of letting an incautious word slip through momentary carelessness.

'*We are quite used to the idea of people in hiding or "underground," as in bygone days one was used to Daddy's bedroom slippers warming in front of the fire. There are a great number of*

From left to right:
Bep Voskuijl,
Johannes Kleiman,
Victor Kugler and
Miep Gies.

organizations such as "The Free Netherlands" which forge identity cards, hand out money to peo-
ple "underground," find hiding places for people, and work for young men in hiding, and it is
amazing how much noble, unselfish work these people are doing, risking their own lives to help
and save others. Our helpers are a very good example, they have pulled us through up till now
and we hope they will bring us safely to dry land. Otherwise they would have to share the same
fate as the many others who are being searched for. Never have we heard one word of the burden
which we certainly must be to them, never has one of them complained about all the trouble we
cause. They all come upstairs every day, talk to the men about business and politics, to the women
about food and wartime difficulties, and about newspapers and books with the children.'
(28 January 1944)

The diary

For about two years, Anne wrote of events in the Secret Annexe in her diary. In the
beginning she mainly reported daily incidents. After a number of weeks, she changed
her writing style. In her letters to Kitty, a make-believe friend, Anne began to write
more and more about her own feelings and personal development. It also appeared
that information from the outside regularly made its way into the shielded Secret
Annexe. So Anne reported on 9 October 1942: '*I've only got dismal and depressing news for*
you today. Our many Jewish friends are being rounded up by the dozen. These people are treated by
the Gestapo without a shred of decency, being loaded into cattle trucks and sent to Westerbork, the
big Jewish camp in Drente. Miep told us about a man who escaped from Westerbork. Westerbork
sounds terrible. People get hardly anything to eat let alone drink, for they have water for only one
hour a day and one w.c. and one washstand for a few thousand people. (. . .) If it is as bad as
this in Holland, whatever will it be like in the distant and barbarous regions they are sent to? We
assume that most of them are murdered. The English radio speaks of their being gassed; perhaps
that is the quickest way to die. I feel terribly upset.'

On 19 November 1942, after Dussel's arrival, she wrote about news he had brought

Anne's first diary, which she received on her thirteenth birthday, 12 June 1942.

from the 'outside world': *He had very sad news. Countless friends and acquaintances have gone to a terrible end. Evening after evening the green and grey army lorries trundle past and ring at every front door to inquire if there are any Jews living in the house. If there are, then the whole family has to go at once. If they don't find any they go on to the next house. No one has a chance of evading them, unless one goes into hiding. (. . .) In the evenings when it's dark, I often see rows of good, innocent people accompanied by crying children, walking on and on, in the charge of a couple of these chaps, bullied and knocked about until they almost drop. Nobody is spared, old people, children, babies, expectant mothers, the sick each and all join in the march of death.'*

Anne could not shut out the continuing war and persecution of the Jews. Now and then she wrote about the guilt which overcame her whenever she realized what others were going through. In the same letter from 19 November 1942, she wrote: *'I feel wicked sleeping in a warm bed, while my dearest friends have been knocked down or have fallen into a gutter somewhere out in the cold night.'* A few weeks later she wrote: *'And as for us, we are fortunate. Yes, we are luckier than millions of people. It is quiet and safe here, and we are, so to speak, living on capital.'* (13 January 1943).

A few months later she described the latest anti-Jewish measures: *'Rauter, one of the German big shots, has made a speech. "All Jews must be out of the German-occupied countries by July 1. Between April 1 and May 1 the province of Utrecht must be cleaned out (as if the Jews were cockroaches), between May 1 to June 1 the provinces of North and South Holland." These wretched people are sent to filthy slaughterhouses like a herd of poor sick, neglected cattle. But I won't talk about it, I only get nightmares from such thoughts!'* (27 March 1943).

Reports from the outside reached the inhabitants of the Secret Annexe through the helpers and through the radio. There was a radio in the 'private office' on the first floor of the back annexe. After six o'clock in the evening, when the building was empty, the upstairs inhabitants regularly came down to listen to the radio. The most important, of course, was news from the BBC and Radio Oranje, the free station

Waterlooplein: one of the entrances to the Jewish quarter in Amsterdam.

Jews with their baggage waiting for transport.

Amsterdam, summer 1943: an illegally-made photograph of Jews on their way to the train bound for Westerbork.

broadcast by the Dutch government in exile in London. At the end of July 1943, all radios in the Netherlands had to be handed in by order of the Germans. As a replacement, Kleiman brought in a 'baby radio' which was put in the back annexe. In this way they learned about the capitulation of Italy on 8 September 1943. In Anne's words: '*The Dutch programme from England began at a quarter past eight. "Listeners, one and a quarter hours ago I had just finished writing the chronicle of the day when the wonderful news of Italy's capitulation came in. I can tell you that I have never deposited my notes in the wastepaper basket with such joy!" "God Save the King," the American national anthem and the Russian "Internationale" were played. As always, the Dutch program was uplifting, but not too optimistic.*'

After January 1944 an important part of Anne's diary was occupied by her friendship with Peter. She discovered in him someone with whom she could talk about her feelings, and they gradually fell in love. This offered both of them the opportunity to isolate themselves from the other inhabitants of the Secret Annexe. Their meeting places were Peter's little room and the attic. On February 18, Anne wrote: '*Whenever I go upstairs now, I keep hoping that I shall see "him." Because my life now has some object and I have something to look forward to, everything has become more pleasant. At least the object of my feelings is always there, and I needn't be afraid of rivals (except Margot).*' Naturally, in the small Secret Annexe community this gave rise to occasional jokes and teasing. Anne's diary shows, however, that both she and Peter could hold their own against it.

Another important development in Anne's life, which was directly related to her diary, is that in the course of the spring of 1944 she decided that later she wanted to become a writer. Her infatuation with Peter was not the only thing on her mind. On Wednesday, April 5, she wrote: '*Peter filled my days – nothing but Peter, dreams and thoughts until Saturday night, when I felt so utterly miserable; oh, it was terrible. (. . .) And now it's all over, I must work, so as not to be a fool, to get on to become a journalist, because that's what I want! I know that I can write. (. . .) I can shake off everything if I write; my sorrows disappear,*

The stairway in Peter's room going to the Annexe's attic.

The old arched window in the Annexe's attic with view of the Westerkerk tower: the only way to look at the sky without risk.

my courage is reborn! But, and that is the great question, will I ever be able to write anything great, will I ever become a journalist or a writer? ' Anne had already been writing short stories for some time in a separate notebook which she called 'the story book'.

On 28 March 1944, Minister Bolkestein, member of the Dutch government in exile, spoke on Radio Oranje: '*History cannot be written on the basis of official decisions and documents alone. If our descendants are to understand fully what we as a nation have had to endure and overcome during these years, then what we really need are ordinary documents – a diary, letters from a worker in Germany, a collection of sermons given by a parson or a priest. Not until we succeed in bringing together vast quantities of this simple, everyday material will the picture of our struggle for freedom be painted in its full depth and glory.*' This speech gave Anne reason to revise her diary. On 11 May 1944, she wrote: '*In any case, I want to publish a book entitled* Het Achterhuis *after the war, whether I shall succeed or not, I cannot say, but my diary will be a great help.*' About a week later, after '*a great deal of reflection*', she began to

52 rewrite her first diary. She changed the style, dropped passages which she found less important, added bits that the future reader might find interesting and invented other names for the Secret Annexe inhabitants and the helpers. The names Van Daan, Dussel, Koophuis, Kraler – which later would sound so familiar to millions – came into being at that time. Anne rewrote her diary on loose sheets of copy paper and must have put many weeks of hard work into the task. She was not able to finish. The rewriting ended with the entry for 29 March 1944.

Anne's notes from the last weeks in the Secret Annexe give witness to the general sense of optimism. Spirits rose with the reports of the Allied invasion of Normandy on D-Day. '*Great commotion in the Secret Annexe! Would the long-awaited liberation about which so much has been said, but which still seems too wonderful, too much like a fairy tale, ever come true? Could we be granted victory this year, this 1944? We don't know yet, but hope lives on; it gives us fresh courage, it makes us strong again.*' This Anne wrote on Tuesday, 6 June 1944, a few days before her fifteenth birthday. With the successes of the Allied troops in

Reconstruction of the
Van Daan family's
room.

A part of Anne's collected works. A photo album with texts in her hand has also been saved.

First page of Anne's last, unfinished diary: *'from 17 April 1944, to … '*.

France, the hopes of the group in hiding rose by the day. The assassination attempt on Hitler's life, made on July 20, produced real cheer in the Secret Annexe. Anne entitled the report 'Super news'. Despite the fact that the attack failed, it was a sign for everyone that the resistance was increasing in Germany as well. The last diary entry which we have from Anne is dated August 1. It does not describe recent events in the Secret Annexe, nor does it report news from the outside. In her last notes, Anne looked within and ruminated on the difference between her inner world and the outer self which she believed emanated from her. *'I know exactly how I'd like to be, how I am too . . . inside. But alas I'm only like that for myself. And perhaps that's why, no I'm sure it's the reason why I say I've got a happy nature within and why other people think I've got a happy nature without. I am guided by the pure Anne within, but outside I'm nothing but a frolicsome little goat who's breaking loose. (. . .) I keep on trying to find a way of becoming what I would so like to be and what I could be, if . . . there weren't any other people living in the world.'* With this Anne's diary ended.

Deportation

Friday, 4 August 1944, was a warm summer day. Nothing that morning indicated that this day would be totally different from any other. The inhabitants of the Secret Annexe kept themselves quiet as usual beginning at eight-thirty and were spread over the various rooms in their hiding place. Otto Frank was upstairs, giving an English lesson to Peter in his little room. At ten-thirty a car appeared in front of the house and a uniformed man got out accompanied by a few assistants. Later it become known that this was an Austrian Nazi named Silberbauer. Inside the office he asked Kugler to show him the building. When they came to the landing it became clear that the group in hiding had been betrayed. Silberbauer and his assistants seemed to be completely

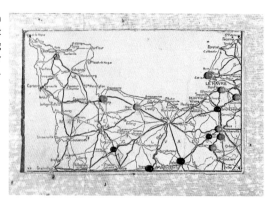

Map of Normandy on which Otto Frank kept track of the advancing Allied troops after D-Day.

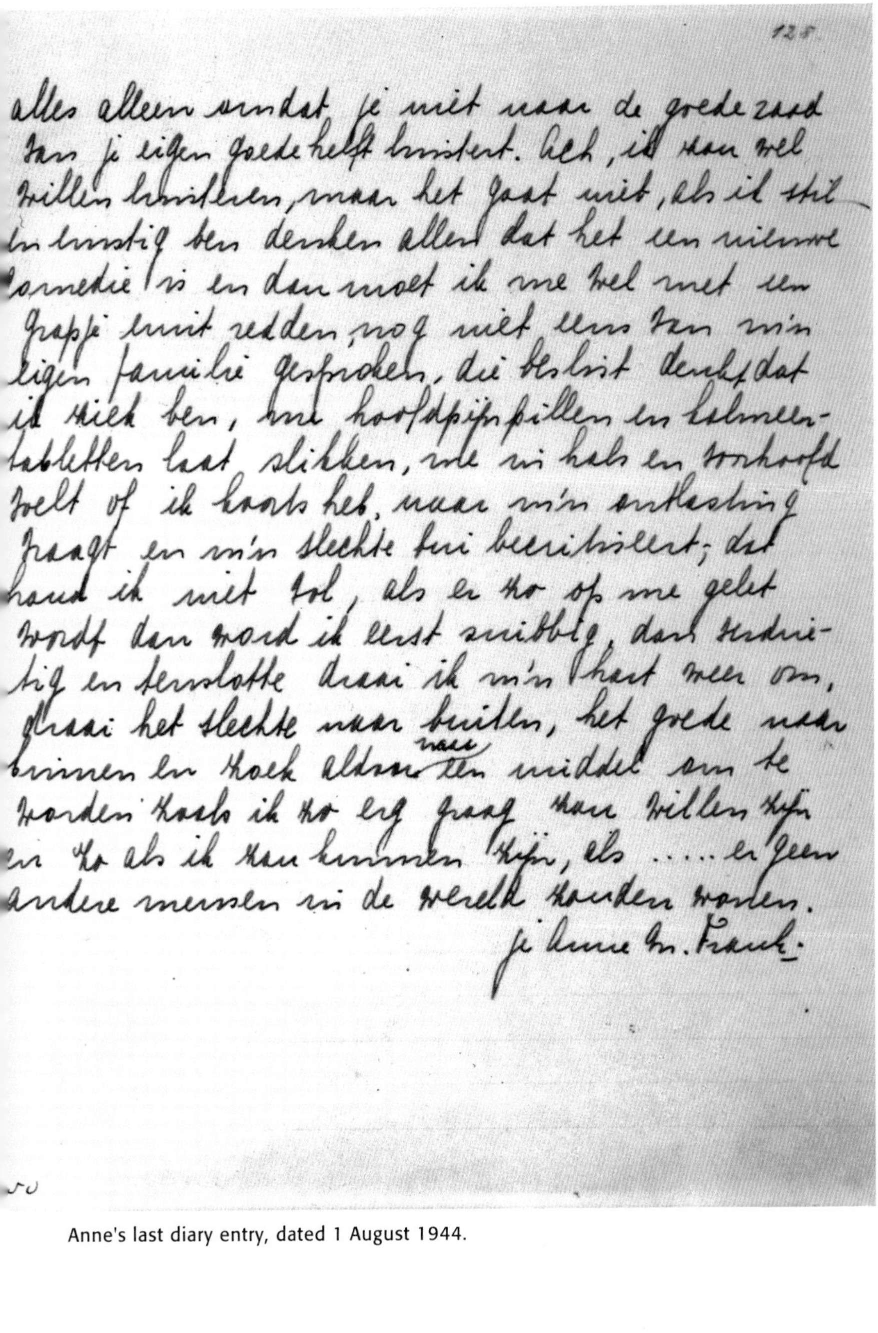
125.

alles alleen omdat je niet naar de goede raad van je eigen goede helft luistert. Ach, ik zou wel willen luisteren, maar het gaat niet, als ik stil en ernstig ben denken allen dat het een nieuwe comedie is en dan moet ik me wel met een grapje eruit redden, nog niet eens van m'n eigen familie gesproken, die beslist denkt dat ik ziek ben, me hoofdpijnpillen en kalmeertabletten laat slikken, me in hals en voorhoofd voelt of ik koorts heb, naar m'n ontlasting vraagt en m'n slechte bui bekritiseert; dat houd ik niet vol, als er zo op me gelet wordt dan word ik eerst snibbig, dan verdrietig en tenslotte draai ik m'n hart weer om, draai het slechte naar buiten, het goede naar binnen en zoek aldoor naar een middel om te worden zoals ik zo erg graag zou willen zijn en zo als ik zou kunnen zijn, als ... er geen andere mensen in de wereld zouden wonen.

je Anne M. Frank.

50

Anne's last diary entry, dated 1 August 1944.

informed about the secret door and forced Kugler to push the bookcase aside. Kugler then had to lead them up to the terrified inhabitants. The group was ordered at gunpoint to gather in the Frank family's room while the Dutch assistants searched the other rooms. Any money or jewelry had to be handed over. Silberbauer picked up Otto Frank's briefcase, where Anne kept her papers and diary entries. He shook the papers onto the floor and replaced them with his booty. So Anne's diary remained behind.

While waiting for a larger vehicle to take away the group in hiding, Silberbauer continued to look round the room and spotted Otto's empty army chest imprinted with his name and rank. His attitude changed immediately. The group were allowed to take their time to pack some clothing and toilet articles.

At about one o'clock the vehicle arrived and took away the eight inhabitants of the Secret Annexe plus Kleiman and Kugler. These last two spent about a month in an Amsterdam House of Detention, after which they were sent to Camp Amersfoort. Four days after their arrest, the group of eight were brought to the Westerbork transit camp in the eastern part of the Netherlands. From here, for almost two years since 1942, weekly trains had departed for the extermination camps, specifically Auschwitz and Sobibor in Poland. On September 3 (the south of the Netherlands had already been liberated by the Allies), the last transport left Westerbork. Among the 1011 people were the eight who had been in hiding together. They arrived in Auschwitz on the night of September 5-6.

A definite identification of the person ultimately responsible for the betrayal of the eight inhabitants of the Annexe has never been determined. For the helpers left behind, it was certain that betrayal was involved: indeed, for two years everything had gone well. Virtually all suspicion fell on the warehouse employee Van Maaren, the successor of Bep's father, Voskuijl. Van Maaren had been hired in the spring of 1943. As time went by, he became more and more curious and suspicious. Anne wrote about

In the Westerbork transit camp.

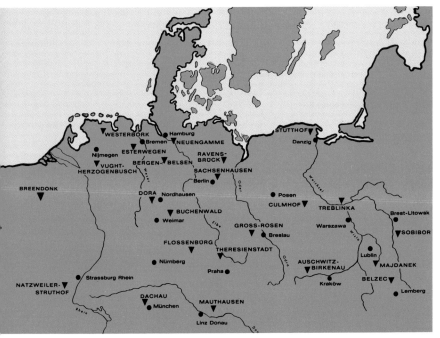

Central Europe, with the most important concentration camps and extermination camps.

Sign on the railroad carriages bound for Auschwitz: 'Do not uncouple the carriages; the entire train must return to Westerbork intact'.

various incidents, among them some burglaries of which Van Maaren was suspected. After the war in 1948, an investigation of the betrayal was made. Van Maaren was also cross-examined, but nothing could be proved. In 1963 the case was again opened when Silberbauer was tracked down in that year. In addition to new witnesses, Van Maaren was questioned again. This investigation also failed to lead to any concrete results. It is still possible that he played the dubious role of betrayer. It also could have been someone else who became aware of the hiding place either accidentally or through rumours. The truth will probably never be known.

The Annexe abandoned

Miep and Bep could never forget that first Friday in August 1944. After more than two years spent caring for the group of eight in hiding it all suddenly seemed to have been in vain. Later that afternoon, Miep, accompanied by her husband Jan, Bep and the head warehouse employee, went to the Annexe to size up the situation. In the chaos they found Anne's papers lying on the floor. Miep stored them in her desk, under lock and key. They also took a few other articles which were of value to the former inhabitants of the Secret Annexe, hoping to be able to give them back later. Within two weeks, the Puls removal firm, under orders of the Germans, came to empty the Secret Annexe. This was 'normal' practice wherever Jews were found and taken away. Usually their effects were traded or transported to Germany.

After the weekend, Miep tried to buy the freedom of the former Annexe inhabitants and even went to the headquarters of the German police. It was, however, to no avail: while she was making this attempt the eight were already on their way to Westerbork.

Although it sounds odd, business at the Prinsengracht continued as usual. Miep and Bep took over Kugler and Kleiman's work, and work in the warehouse also continued with its normal routine. Kleiman became ill at Camp Amersfoort. Through the intervention of the Red Cross he was allowed to return home in September. At the end

Lorries from Puls, the removal company that emptied the Annexe for the Germans.

JUDENTRANSPORT AUS DEN NIEDERLANDEN - LAGER WESTERBORK

Haeftlinge

301.✓Engers	Isidor — ✓30.4.	93 -	Kaufmann
302✓ Engers	Leonard	15.6.	20 -	Lamdarbeiter
303✓ Franco	Manfred - ✓1.5.	05 -	Verleger
304. Frank	Arthur	22.8.	81	Kaufmann
305. Frank ×	Isaac	✓29.11.87		Installateur
306. Frank	Margot	.16.2. 26		ohne
307. Frank ✓	Otto	✓12.5. 89		Kaufmann
308.✓ Frank-Hollaender	Edith	16.1. 00		ohne
309. Frank	Anneliese	12.6. 29		ohne
310. v.Franck	Sara -	27.4. 82-		Typistin
311. Franken	Rozanna	16.5. 96-		Landarbeiter
312.✓ Franken-Weyand	Johanna	24.12.96►		Landbauer
313. Franken	Hermann - ✓12.5.34		ohne
314. Franken	Louis	10.8. 17-		Gaertner
315. Franken ℛ	Rosalina	29.3. 27		Landbau
316. Frankfort	Alex	14.11.19-		Dr.i.d.Oekonomie
317. Frankfort-Elsas	Regina	11.12.19		Apoth-.Ass.
318. Frankfoort ×	Elias	✓22.10.98-		Schneider
319.✓Frankfort ℛ	Max	20.6. 21		Schneider
320.✓Frankfort-Weijl ℛ	Hetty	29.3. 24		Naeherin
321.✓Frankfort-Werkendam Rosette	24.6.98		Schriftstellerin
322.✓Frijda	Hermann	22.6. 87-		Hochschullehrer
323. Frenk	Henriette	28.4. 21		Typistin
324. Frenk ℛ	Rosa	15.3.24		Haushalthilfe
325. Friezer	Isaac	10.3. 20 -		Korrespondent
326.✓ Fruitman-Vlessche-			
drager Fanny	24.1. 03		ohne
327. Gans ×	Elie	✓24.10.03-		Betriebleiter
328. Gans-Koopman ℛ	Gesina	20.12.05		Maschinestrickerin
329. Gans	Kalman —	6.3. 79		Diamantarbeiter
330. Gans ℛ .	Klara	12.5. 13		Naeherin
331. Gans ·	Paul —	27.9. 08 -		Landbauer
332. v.Gelder	Abraham -	9.11.78		Metzger
2. 333. v.Gelder-de Jong	Reintje	22.10.81		ohne
334. v.Gelder	Alexander	27.6. 03 -		Kaufmann
335. v.Gelder-Visch-			
schraper× Clara	12.4. 12		ohne
336. v.Gelder-Raphael× Hendrika	17.3. 77		ohne
337. v.Gelder ℛ	Henny	15.5. 18		Naeherin
338. v.Gelder	Simon —	✓19.5. 19-		Landarbeiter
339. v.Gelderen ✓	Johanna	22.3. 10 -		Verkaeuferin
340. v.Gelderen ↙	Karel -	25.6. 99-		Kapellmeister
341. Gerson	Alexander	1.5. 69		ohne
342. Gersons-Hartog	Kaatje	29.9. 94		ohne
? 343. Ginsberg ℛ	Arthur	►24.3. 27-		Baecker
• 344. Ginsberg	Benjamin -,7.9. 93-		Kaufmann
345. Ginsberg-Rosen	Rosa	10.6. 97-		ohne
346. Glowinski ×	Israel	✓3.5. 94-		Stepper
347✓ Glowinski-Streep	Sara	31.12.91		Naeherin

Part of the transport list from the last train leaving Westerbork for Auschwitz.

of October, he returned to the Prinsengracht and took over the direction of the business. The back Annexe served no further function and remained empty.

The fate of the Annexe's inhabitants

Mrs Frank died in Auschwitz of hunger and exhaustion on 6 January 1945. Mr van Daan was gassed a few weeks after his arrival in the camp. Mrs van Daan was taken to Theresienstadt in April 1945, by way of Auschwitz, Bergen-Belsen and Buchenwald. From there she was transported again, but the destination is not known. She did not survive the war either. On 16 January 1945 when the Russian troops were approaching and the liberation of the camp was at hand, Peter was taken away with thousands of others. In these so-called 'death marches' the prisoners were forced to walk vast distances every day, westward, away from the advancing Russian army. Peter finally arrived in Mauthausen, where he died on 5 May 1945. Dussel was also transported from Auschwitz. He died on 20 December 1944 in the concentration camp at Neuengamme. At the end of October, Anne and Margot were transported to Bergen-Belsen when Auschwitz was evacuated. This camp, which lay on the Lüneburg Heath below Hannover, served as a sort of collection camp during those months. Because many more people arrived there than the camp was built to accommodate, the conditions that winter became abominable: hardly any food, insufficient shelter in the fierce cold and a total absence of hygienic measures. The prisoners were completely left to their own fates. A typhus epidemic broke out which took the lives of tens of thousands, among them Margot and Anne. Both probably died at the beginning of March 1945 only a few weeks before the liberation of the camp by the British.

Otto Frank was the sole member of the group to survive the war. When the death marches began he remained in one of the hospital barracks in Auschwitz. He was liberated, along with the other prisoners left behind, by the Russians on 27 January 1945. After a long train journey he arrived in Odessa, the harbour city on the Black Sea.

The entrance to Auschwitz-Birkenau.

Pages 62–63: a mass grave in Bergen-Belsen,
the camp where Anne and Margot died in March 1945.

From there he continued further by ship to Marseilles. On June 3 Otto returned to
Amsterdam. He moved in with Miep and Jan Gies and would stay with them for several
years.

Otto Frank's ticket for Marseilles to the Netherlands. The destination
given in Amsterdam is the address of Miep and Jan Gies.

Events surrounding the diary

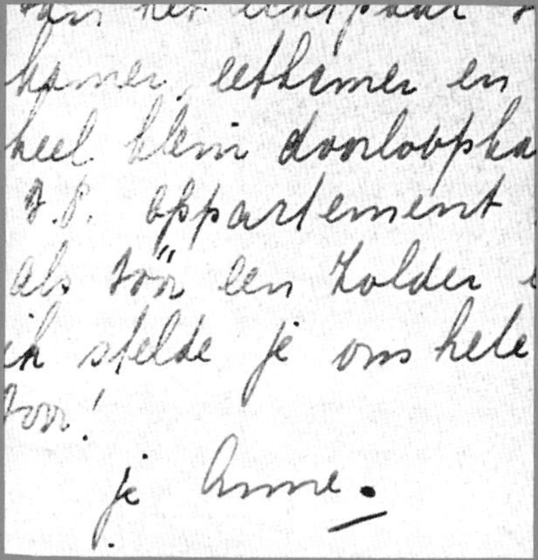
kamer, eetkamer en
heel klein doorloopka
P.S. appartement
als ook een zolder
ik stelde je ons hele
voor!
je Anne.

I n the newly-liberated Netherlands, the war was still noticeable everywhere during the summer of 1945. For many the liberation had come too late. More than one hundred thousand Dutch Jews did not survive the war. However, the fate of many was still unknown during those first months.

By then Otto knew that his wife had died in Auschwitz, but he still had hope that Anne and Margot were alive. He placed a search advertisement in the newspaper as many others were doing in the hope that someone would respond. After several weeks, around the beginning of August, he was informed that his daughters would not be returning either. He was assured of this by prisoners from Bergen-Belsen who had been with Anne and Margot during their last days. Only then did Miep give him, as she herself put it, '*the legacy from his daughter*'. This took place in the office on the Prinsengracht, where Otto had resumed his function as director after his return to Amsterdam. He took all of Anne's manuscripts to his old private office one floor beneath the hiding place and immediately began to read them. Later he took the first diary and the other completed notebooks and loose sheets back with him to Miep and Jan's house.

In the weeks that followed, Otto began typing out those parts of Anne's diary that were most meaningful to him in order to share them with family members and friends. He translated parts of the text into German for his mother, who lived in Switzerland. Shortly afterward he made a more complete copy of the diary, using Anne's second version as a basis. He edited all the entries to create one running whole. In this way 'Het Achterhuis' took shape, the book that Anne herself had envisioned. This was no invented novel but a report of actual events which Otto made available to an ever-expanding group of friends and acquaintances.

In the office, October 1945. From left to right, Miep Gies, Johannes Kleiman, Otto Frank, Victor Kugler and Bep Voskuijl.

INLICHTINGEN GEVRAAGD OMTRENT

JAN DIRK FLASCHWINKEL, geb. 10-3-'94 loodgieter, laatst bek. verblijfplaats Amersfoort No. 1413 blok 8, verm. begin Oct. n. Duitsland vervoerd. Mevr. Flaschwinkel, Wouwermanstraat 36, Haarlem.

JAN SCHREUDER, geb. 29-11-'94. Tot Sept. in Vught, blok 17A. Daarna naar Oranienburg. W. J. Schreuder, Planetenplein 9, Haarlem.

THEO BERGEN, laatste verblijfplaats Gemeinschaftslager 2 KHD Oberursel/Taunus bij Frankfort a.d. Main. Bergen, Pluvierstr. 10, A'dam-N

MARTIN HOLLEMAN, geb. 19-10-1917. Laatst gewoond hebbende Arndstrasse 26a te Magdeburg. Zij die hem na de capitulatie gezien of gesproken hebben schrijven aan fam. J. Holleman, Beekkade 13 Hillegom.

HEYMAN CONTENT (geb. 4-3-'92), gewoond hebb. Sarphatistraa 207, A'dam, later Reitzstraat 43. Oct. 1943 in Westerbork, barak 62. Porto w. gaarne vergoed. Br. CANTON. Postbox 658, A'dam.

MEYER VAN LEEUWEN, geb. 1-11-1870. D. VAN LEEUWEN—BERLIJN, geb. 27-6-1880. 1 Febr. '43 van Westerbork. ABR. v. LEEUWEN, geb. 3 Jan. '08. E. E. v. LEEUWEN—VAN LIER, geb. 26-8-'10. 13-7-'43 v. W. allen verm. Auschwitz. R. DE GROOT—v. LEEUWEN, Amaliastraat 18, II, A'dam.

IRMA SPIELMANN, geb. 10-4-'94 Wenen, Tsj. Slow. nation. Weggevoerd Westerborg 23-3-'43. Wie weet iets van dit transport? Spielmann, Scheldestr. 181 III, Zuid.

MARGOT FRANK (19 j.) en **ANNA FRANK** (16 j.), in Jan. op transp. vanuit Bergen-Belzen. O. Frank, Prinsengracht 263, tel. 37059.

Mijn man **ALFRED v. GELDEREN**. (Oct. 1942 uit Westerb.) en kinderen **DORA ROSA** en **FREDERIK MARTHIJN** (24-7-1942 uit Westerb.) Marianne v. Gelderen—Engelander, Jozef Israëlkade 126 II.

FRANCISCUS JOHANNES MAAS geb. 19-10-'23, werkz. bij Machinefabriek Winger en Co. Waltersdorf Kreis Zittau Saksen Duitsland. Inl. gevr. van hen, die hem na 16 Sept. 1944 hebben gezien. J. Ch. H. Maas, Kamperfoelieweg 16, A'dam-N.

COR v. RENSSEN, geb. 6-6-'24, wonende te Delft, laatste adres Wiesenstrasse Babelsberg-Potsdam. D. T. v. LOO, Durbanstraat 58, Den Haag.

WILLEM v. d. POL, 42 j. Laatst ontvangen mededeling van collega's in Januari 1944 op fabriek Siemens & Halske, Berlijn gearresteerd en weggevoerd. Nadien nimmer iets vernomen. M. P. v. d. POL—VOGEL, W. de Zwijgerlaan 269, A'dam.

FAMILIE WILLI KAN, 3-6-'98. SUSIE KAN—v. MINDEN, geb. 25-9-'04 en hun kinderen **DANNY RALPH** en **BETSY**, vertrokken uit Bergen Belsen ongeveer Oct.-Nov. 1944 en vermoedelijk gedeporteerd in de

Among the many search advertisements which appeared in Dutch newspapers in 1945 is one from Otto Frank.

First publication

The first serious notion to find a publisher for the diary occurred in the beginning of 1946. There was little interest, however, during the first post-war year in reminders of that black period. It was time to look forward, not backward, and sights were set on the future and the rebuilding of the Netherlands. Another stumbling block for a few publishers was the highly personal nature of the diary and the passages describing Anne's early sexuality. Finally it was Jan Romein, a well-known Dutch historian, who made the breakthrough. He had been given the manuscript and was deeply stirred. On 3 April 1946 he wrote a review which appeared in the daily newspaper 'Het Parool' under the title 'A Child's Voice': '*By chance a diary written during the war years has come into my possession. The Netherlands State Institute for War Documentation already holds some two hundred similar diaries, but I should be very much surprised if there were another as lucid, as intelligent, and at the same time as natural. This one made me forget the present and its many calls to duty for a whole evening as I read it from beginning to end. When I had finished it was nighttime, and I was astonished to find that the lights still worked, that we still had bread and tea, that I could hear no airplanes droning overhead and no pounding of army boots in the street – I had been so engrossed in my reading, so carried away back to that unreal world, now almost a year behind us. (. . .) If all the signs do not deceive me, this girl would have become a talented writer had she remained alive.*' It was the article in Het Parool that ignited the interest of the Amsterdam publisher Contact, and the manuscript was delivered to them via a friend of Otto Frank. That summer Contact agreed to publish the diary. During the following months the text was prepared for printing. With the two versions that Anne had written plus all the other texts which actually belonged to the diary as well, this process proved to be complicated and lengthy. In addition, the publisher made certain changes in the text, not only in style and word choice but also in the exclusion of parts which were not considered 'suitable' at that time. Although this editing produced a diary which was less than a direct transcription of Anne's chronicle, for Otto the essence still

Het Parool, 3 April 1946. The first article about the diary appeared under the title 'A Child's Voice'.

Red. en Adm.: A'dam-C.
N.Z. Voorburgwal 225.
Tel. 36232. Gem.G. P10.500
Postgiro no. 260728.
Ab. 31 ct. p. w. of f 4 p. kw
Losse nummers 9 cent
Bankierss Amst. Bank N.V.,
Bijkantoor Damrak.

HET PAROOL

VRIJ, ONVERVEERD

ONAFHANKELIJK
DAGBLAD
Uitgave van de Stichting
Het Parool, Amsterdam
Opgericht in 1940 door
PIETER 't HOEN.
Directeur W. v. NORDEN

ZESDE JAARGANG No. 378 — Hoofdredacteur: Mr. G. J. van Heuven Goedhart. — WOENSDAG 3 APRIL 1946

Kinderstem

DOOR een toeval heb ik een dagboek in handen gekregen, dat tijdens de oorlogsjaren geschreven is. Het Rijksinstituut voor Oorlogsdocumenta, te bezit al omtrent 200 dergelijke dagboeken, maar het zou mij verbazen, als er daar nog één bij was, zóó zuiver, zóó intelligent, en toch zoo menschelijk als dit, dat ik hen heden met zijn vele plichten voor één avond vergetend, in eenen gelezen heb.

Toen ik het las, was het nacht en het verwonderde mij, dat het licht nog brandde, dat er nog brood en thee te krijgen waren, dat ik geen vliegtuigen hoorde ronken en geen soldaten laarzen klonken op straat, zóó had de lezing mij bevangen en teruggevoerd naar de onwezenlijke wereld, die en al bijna weer om jaar achter ons ligt.

NA ZEVEN JAAR WEER JAARBEURS IN UTRECHT.

Duizenden waren gisteren, den dag der opening, aanwezig om deze heuglijke gebeurtenis in het Nederlandsche bedrijfsleven bij te wonen.

ER WORDEN WEER ORDERS GENOTEERD aan de stands op de Jaarbeurs in Utrecht.

Ir. Müller staat Vrijdag terecht

De F. E. Müller, die tijdens de bezetting burgemeester van Rotterdam was, zal Vrijdag a.s. terechtstaan in de openbare zitting van het Bijzondere Gerechtshof te 's-Gravenhage, te behandelen in het ...

Engelsche anti-stakingswet thans ingetrokken

ONDER daverende en langdurige toejuichingen van de afgevaardigden der Arbeiderspartij heeft het Engelsche Lagerhuis met 314 tegen 187 stemmen de private „Trades Disputes Act" ingetrokken, welke een algemeene staking onwettig verklaarde en het financiering van de vakvereenigingen en de Arbeiderspartij voor ambtenaren verbood.

De Bilt verwacht:

tot Donderdagavond: Helderen nacht met weinig wind, hier en daar lichten ochtendnevel. Overdag tot matig toenemenden wind tusschen Zuid-Oost en Zuid-West. In den middag, vooral in het Westen van het land, eenige lichte bewolking. Zacht weer.
Zon onder 19.15, op 6.09
Maan op 7.12, onder 21.06
8 April E.K.

Zuivering bestuur der P.T.T.

Onlangs vermeldden wij, dat de Commissie-Westerveld, belast met het uitbrengen van advies in zake de zuivering van het P.T.T-personeel, geconcludeerd had tot volledige rehabilitatie van de hoofdbestuursambtenaren Harting, Bosma en mej. Verachoor, doch dat aan deze conclusie door den Directeur-Generaal der P.T.T. geenerlei uitvoering is gegeven.

DEZEN ZOMER OPROEPING NIEUWE LICHTINGEN

In Mei en October zullen de lichtingen 1945 en 1946 onder de wapenen worden geroepen, in totaal ter sterkte van ongeveer 60.000 man, alles heeft de minister van Oorlog, J. Meynen, in zijn antwoord op de vragen van het Tweede-Kamerlid L. F. Duymaer van Twist verklaard.

KAARSEN VRIJ.

Kaarsen zullen voortaan weder zonder bon in den detailhandel verkrijgbaar zijn, zij het nog niet in onbeperkte hoeveelheden.

Oproep van Partij van den Arbeid

De Partij van den Arbeid heeft zich met een Oproep tot het Nederlandsche volk gericht in verband met de komende a.s. verkiezingen voor de Tweede Kamer, Provinciale Staten en gemeenteraden.

Met Paschen een ei

Op 8 April a.s. zal voor Paschen een bon voor een ei zeker beschikbaar worden gesteld, welke bon geldig zal blijven.

Duinbrand bij Zandvoort

In de duinen ter hoogte van het Badstation te Zandvoort is gistermiddag om ongeveer 4 uur brand ontstaan.

Prof. dr. S. de Boer berispt

De minister van O. K. en W. heeft prof. dr. S. de Boer berispt wegens zijn houding gedurende de bezetting en zijn scherpen aanval op de hoogleeraar van de Vrije Universiteit.

Veiligheidsraad heden bijeen

Bonnet bemiddelaar?

(News Chronicle — Het Parool).
BYRNES werd gisteravond laat uit Washington, waar hij een onderhoud van een uur met President Truman had in New York terug verwacht.

RUIMERE OPLEIDING VOOR TANDARTSEN

Faculteit aanbevolen in Amsterdam en Groningen

De staatscommissie, die in October 1945 door den minister werd ingesteld om met spoed een reorganisatie van het lager onderwijs in de tandheelkunde voor te stellen.

Regeeringsvertegenwoordiger bij de Unilever

Goeden Vrijdag wordt doorgewerkt

De minister-president heeft besloten, dat op Goeden Vrijdag a.s. op alle departementen en algemeen bureaux als op gewone werkdag zal worden gewerkt.

Sjahrir en Kerr uiten zich beiden optimistisch

SJAHRIR heeft in een interview, dat hij gisteren volgens A.N.P.Aneta toestond aan de plaatselijke bladen in Batavia, zijn voldoening uitgesproken over de vorderingen, die tot dusver bij de onderhandelingen met de Nederlanders zijn gemaakt, maar hij wees er op, dat nog veel vereikegeld moet worden.

J. ROMEIN

DE EVACUATIE VAN IRAN door de Russische troepen gaat met onverminderde snelheid voort. De stad Mejid in Oost-Iran was der eerste plaatsen, die door de Sovjet-legers, voorafgegaan door cavalerie, begin Maart werden ontruimd.

remained: reason enough for him to agree to the changes. In June 1947, two years after the war ended, the diary was published under the title 'Het Achterhuis', the name for the book which Anne herself had invented. The first printing was 1500 copies.

The distribution of the diary

Immediately after publication, the diary received high critical praise in various dailies and weeklies. A reprint was inevitable. Interest in the book began to appear in foreign countries as well. In 1950 in Germany and France the first translations came on the market. Two years later the English translation of the diary appeared and was also published in the United States. Eleanor Roosevelt, the widow of the former American president, wrote a foreword for this edition. It wasn't only in America where the book struck a chord; dozens of other countries followed. In the last forty years it has become the most widely translated Dutch book. Undoubtedly, the success of the play and the film has been a contributing factor.

After an earlier, unsuccessful attempt to adapt the diary to the stage, the couple Albert Hackett and Frances Goodrich worked the book into a play. It premiered in New York in 1955 and was performed in several European countries during the following year. The play made a deep impression at that time, although audience reactions varied widely. Sometimes the public gave a long standing ovation; at other times there was complete silence in the theatre after the play ended. In 1957 the play was made into a Hollywood film. The interior of the Secret Annexe was reconstructed in the studio for this purpose. The outside shots, however, were filmed in Amsterdam. Through the play and film, 'Het Achterhuis' was able to reach a new, young audience. This is particularly apparent from the many letters which Otto Frank received during those years from every quarter of the globe.

The motion picture 'The Diary of Anne Frank', directed by George Stevens, has been seen by countless people all over the world after its première.

ANNE FRANK

ANNE
FRANK

Het
Achter-
huis

Het Achter= huis

DAGBOEKBRIEVEN
VAN 14 JUNI 1942 - 1 AUGUSTUS 1944

Cover of the first Dutch edition of the diary.

The diary comes under attack

The international success of Anne's diary also had its dark side, which emerged during the fifties. The growing influence of the diary was a thorn in the flesh for people and groups who tried to give Nazism a better name. There were accusations, especially from neo-Nazi circles in various countries, that the diary was a forgery. In Germany this first occurred in 1958. A teacher, Lothat Stielau of Lübeck, writing in a former students' publication, called the diary '*hardly more authentic* ' than the forged diaries of Eva Braun (Hitler's mistress who, shortly before the fall of Berlin, joined him in marriage and suicide). He was supported by the former Nazi Buddeberg.

In January 1959 Otto Frank and the German publisher of the diary brought criminal charges against the two. A lengthy investigation followed in which not only Otto Frank but also Miep Gies and her husband were cross-examined. Experts scrutinized Anne Frank's handwriting, comparing examples from one diary notebook with that in another. Their report indicated that they had no doubts about the authenticity: all entries were from the same hand, and that was Anne's. Stielau and Buddeberg were cross-examined several times, of course. Stielau later denied that it was the diary that he had referred to; he intended to refer to the stage presentation. When after years of preliminary investigation the court was ready to bring the case to trial, it ended in a settlement. Stielau and Buddeberg regretted their statements and were now convinced of the diary's authenticity. They also declared that Stielau had declared the diary a forgery without reason. The teacher paid a part of the court costs and the case simply petered out. This is regrettable, in retrospect, for now there was no statement from the judge confirming the diary's authenticity, nor was there an official denunciation of the earlier statements. For some, the settlement was not sufficient proof of authenticity, and the imputations continued on into the next year. Most of the attacks could be followed back to the same source: the controversy between Otto Frank and the first playwright to come up with a stage version of the diary, the American Meyer Levin.

Prof. Robert Faurisson

Het Dagboek van Anne Frank: — een vervalsing —

Vrij Historisch Onderzoek

Anne Frank's Diary

A HOAX

by Ditlieb Felderer

Das Tagebuch der Anne Frank

Three publications of French, German and Swedish origin in which the authenticity of the diary is denied, all from after 1975.

The attackers of the diary's authenticity also quoted extensively from each other. In various western European countries as well as in the United States, such opinions were published and continue to be published. In America, for example, the quasi-scientific 'Institute for Historical Review' was active in this area. Next to the allegation that the gas chambers must have been a fabrication, the 'falsification' of the diary is a recurrent theme.

The critical edition

Anne Frank's diary and her other manuscripts remained in Amsterdam until the fifties. When Otto Frank moved to Switzerland he took the diaries with him and had them stored in a bank safe. Only when absolutely necessary, such as for the expert investigation in the case against Stielau, were Anne's papers brought to light. Otto was aware of the value of the papers and was very careful with them. In 1979 he gave out a number of pieces of Anne's legacy on loan to the Anne Frank Stichting. These constitute part of a new exhibition in the attic of the museum, which was opened on the fiftieth anniversary of Anne's birth by the then Queen Juliana. It was Otto's last visit to Amsterdam. In August 1980 he died at the age of 91. In his will he left all his daughter's manuscripts to the government of the Netherlands. A few months later, the first diary and the other completed notebooks and loose sheets came back to the city of their origin, Amsterdam. From that moment, the Netherlands State Institute for War Documentation received the manuscripts in trust.

The Institute quickly planned to proceed with an integral publication of all the diary entries. This would also provide a full picture of the birth of the diary, the differences between Anne's manuscripts and the first published version and the recorded changes in various translations. The preparation of this scientific publication took several years. During that time, handwriting identification and technical document examination were carried out to check for authenticity. To this end handwriting, paper, ink,

12 June 1979: Queen Juliana opens the new exhibition in the Anne Frank House.

glue and the like were thoroughly investigated. Nothing emerged to show that the entries were not original and from Anne's own hand. In 1986 'De Dagboeken van Anne Frank' ('The Diary of Anne Frank: The Critical Edition') was published. Besides an extensive introduction and a summary of the investigation results, this book placed Anne's first version next to her second version and compared the two with 'Het Achterhuis' as it was published in the Netherlands in 1947. Thus an outstanding work was achieved which could ward off attacks on the diary's authenticity or even prevent them. This area of controversy has been quieter in the last years than at the end of the seventies, for example, when doubt was being cast from several corners.

In 1991 the revised and expanded version of 'Het Achterhuis' appeared. In this book, the 1947 publication is reproduced unabridged and supplemented by other passages from Anne's first and second versions. This makes a text which is much more extensive than the version which had been published up until then. One change in the new edition concerns the names of the persons involved. The helpers who are now generally known are indicated by their real names. The pseudonyms which Anne gave to the Van Pels family and Pfeffer are retained, however. We have followed this choice in this text as well.

Anne Frank's list with the pseudonyms she invented.

From canalside house to museum

n 1945 no one could have suspected that the building on the Prinsengracht would be known throughout the world within fifteen years. Just after liberation the Pectacon company was set up again. In addition to Opekta, however, Gies & Co. continued to exist in name so that for a few years three small companies were housed in the building. For a short time after Otto Frank's return, the office staff was the same as it had been in 1942. But two years after the war Miep left her job in order to care for her home and family, as did Bep, who was expecting a baby. Mr Kugler emigrated to Canada at the beginning of 1955, where he died in 1982. Around 1950, after a few painful post-war years, things began to go rather well with Opekta. Kleiman was still director, a post he held until his death in 1959. As the years passed, Otto Frank dedicated more and more of his time to Anne's diary. In 1952, at the age of 63, he moved to Basel in Switzerland where his mother and sister lived. One year later he married Elfriede Markovits, an Auschwitz survivor. She had lost her husband and a son in the war. Her daughter knew Anne from the period when both families lived on the Merwedeplein. In 1953 Otto withdrew permanently from the business, but he continued to visit Amsterdam regularly in the years that followed.

Between 1953 and 1955 the buildings on the corner of the Prinsengracht and the Westermarkt were bought one by one by an estate agent. The owner of 263 Prinsengracht, which still housed the Opekta company, wanted to sell this building to the agent as well. Opekta faced a difficult choice: the building had seriously deteriorated and would have to be renovated completely. Kleiman and Otto Frank were of the opinion that the house should stay in company hands. For this reason, Opekta bought the building in June 1953. But reports from the architectural and construction firm quickly revealed that restoration costs would be enormous.

Another problem was that the planned demolition of the adjacent building would do serious damage to 263 Prinsengracht, whose foundation was extremely weak. The risks were too great and the costs involved in restoration much too high. At the end of

Kleiman and Kugler on the front step of no. 263. The company names are on the door. The photo was taken just after the war.

The outside wall from the Prinsengracht with a view of the Westerkerk tower at the beginning of the fifties.

April 1954 the building was sold, '*with pain in my heart*', said Otto Frank. Opekta was permitted to remain in the building for one year more and moved into a new building in 1955.

Saved from demolition

At the end of 1955 all the buildings on the corner of the Prinsengracht and the Westermarkt became the property of the H. Berghaus First Dutch Ladies' and Children's Coat Factory. This firm intended to demolish all the structures and put up a large office building. The building at 263 Prinsengracht was part of the complex scheduled for demolition.

In the meantime, however, public opinion had been alerted. Newspapers both within the country and abroad announced the threatened demolition and urged that the Secret Annexe be saved. Under the heading '*Anne Frank's Secret Annexe Awaits the Wrecker's Ball*', the daily newspaper Het Vrije Volk reported on 23 November 1955: '*The plan to demolish the Secret Annexe must not continue! If there is one place where the fate of Dutch Jews is most clearly revealed, it is here. The Secret Annexe does not appear on the list of protected monuments, but it nevertheless has become a monument to a time of oppression and man-hunts, terror and darkness. The Netherlands will be subject to a national scandal if this house is indeed pulled down. And is it necessary? The sensible plan would be to allot the property or a small part of it for a small Anne Frank Museum. This has been the actual case for years now. The manuscript of Anne's diary as well as numerous other documents are kept here and shown to visitors. There is every reason, especially considering the enormous interest from both inside and outside the country, to correct this situation as quickly as possible.*'

Since the appearance of the first edition of 'Het Achterhuis' in 1947 people had been coming to the Opekta company to see the former hiding place. Kleiman himself guided them through the building.

End of the fifties, before the restoration: the Anne Frank House in its inception. Visitors must still enter through the small office door.

In Opekta's later years: Mr Kleiman guides the first visitors to the Annexe.

Establishment of the Anne Frank Stichting

The attempt to protect the building from demolition was mounted in every way possible. On 3 May 1957 the Anne Frank Stichting was set up with the aim '*to repair and, where necessary, renovate the property at 263 Prinsengracht in Amsterdam and especially to maintain the building's back annexe, as well as to propagate the ideals left to the world in the diary of Anne Frank*'. The first task of the Stichting was the collection of the necessary funds for the purchase and restoration of the building. It was then that the Berghaus company, on the occasion of its 75th anniversary, donated the building to the Anne Frank Stichting in October 1957. In the meantime, interest in visiting the Secret Annexe had grown so rapidly that the Stichting had to regulate admission. Fixed visiting days and times were established. Visitors were asked to make arrangements beforehand by telephone, after which they were led around the premises. From all over the world the Stichting received expressions of support, and pledges of financial contributions began to come in. This was not unimportant since the building was in need of new foundations.

The plans to demolish the adjacent building remained, however. The intention was to build an eight-storey apartment building on the site, which would change the character of the whole neighbourhood. In the spring of 1958 the board of the Anne Frank Stichting discussed the possibility of including the adjacent building at no. 265 in the restoration plans so that the character of the surrounding neighbourhood could be preserved.

The necessary funds, however, were a large problem. The construction firm which owned the land offered to sell the entire corner plot on the Prinsengracht and the Westermarkt to the Anne Frank Stichting. The board members of the Stichting were necessarily hesitant about this offer: they only wanted to purchase 265 Prinsengracht. Thanks to the cooperation of the then mayor of Amsterdam, Mr G. van Hall, a large-scale collection appeal was started. It was so successful that in October 1958 the Anne

Wreaths in Anne's room after the successes of the play and motion picture. The part of the wallpaper with the movie star collection is cut away for preservation, 1959.

Frank Stichting was able to purchase the entire corner plot. That autumn restoration work on the Anne Frank House began as well.

Plans were made for the restoration and design of 265 Prinsengracht. Conforming to the wishes of Otto Frank, this building would offer space for an international youth centre. An agreement was drawn up with the Students Housing Foundation to design the restored space on the corner of the Prinsengracht and the Westermarkt into a student house. During the summer months, this would be available to the Anne Frank Stichting to offer accommodation to participants in international summer courses and conferences at the Youth Centre.

The official opening

The Anne Frank House was opened on 3 May 1960. On the same day, foundation work was begun on the corner plot for the building of the student house. The restoration of 265 Prinsengracht was in full swing.

In reference to the opening of the Anne Frank House, Otto Frank wrote: '*The intention of the restoration of the house at 263 Prinsengracht was to modernize the front house so that it could be used as an international youth centre, but to leave the back annexe as much as possible in its original condition.*' He described the changes which were introduced in the building. The separating walls in the former warehouse were broken down to produce one large space to be used as a lecture hall. Of the well-known connecting stairway between the first floor and the landing next to the back annexe, Otto Frank wrote: '*This stairway is now closed and can no longer be used because both the building inspectors and the fire department had objections to keeping it open for visitors. This is regrettable, because for those in hiding this stair was the only way to get 'down', of course only before and after working hours and on Sundays. It was also the stairway all the helpers used to come up.*' This stairway is now visible to visitors through a glass plate in the floor. The entrance to the house was changed. To create adequate room downstairs, the stairway which led directly to the

The disused connecting stairway between the first floor and the landing near the Annexe, now still visible through a glass plate in the floor.

office floor was removed. Now the door on the extreme left, with the famous steep stairway behind it, has become the entrance for both the first and second floors.

Otto Frank wrote: '*The back annexe is unchanged. The original swinging book case is still there. It has been made stronger with iron rods. This seemed necessary because the wooden rack was too weak and would have fallen apart with frequent openings. The cushion of wood shavings that Anne wrote about no longer exists: the inside closure is also gone. The wallpaper in the rooms has been replaced with the same pattern as the old, but the part of the old wallpaper where Anne pasted pictures in her room is still there, and the pieces with the map of Normandy and the growth lines of the children are original.*'

The sixties

After the opening of the Anne Frank House, the building at 265 Prinsengracht was restored. The back annexe of this building was to become the office of the Stichting. The large space on the first floor of the front house would become the recreation and meeting room of the youth centre.

The building was opened in May 1961 and the first international youth congress was held with the theme: 'How can young people contribute to better mutual understanding in the world?' Throughout the sixties, many international congresses, cultural demonstrations, lectures and conferences were organized in the Anne Frank House.

Because the Secret Annexe was empty, visitors asked many questions about its earlier layout. For this reason Otto Frank had two models built which showed how the Secret Annexe looked during the period when it served as a hiding place. In 1967 the Anne Frank Stichting celebrated its 10th anniversary. In the annual report the Stichting stated: '*No one in 1957 could have suspected that future visits to the Secret Annexe would assume such proportions: in 1960 about 9000 people visited the house; in 1966 that number had grown to 89,150; in 1967 it was 127,081.*' By 1969 visits had risen to 168,475. Such a large number of visitors had not been envisioned at the time of the restoration in 1959. There were cracks in a number of beams in the front house and back annexe,

Wallpaper in Anne's room with damp spots and streaks of leakage.

Two models made in 1961 with Otto Frank's instructions to give visitors an idea of how the Annexe looked when it was a hiding place.

and the plaster was in urgent need of repair. Traffic flow was a big problem. After visitors had seen the uppermost areas in the back annexe they had to take the steep stairway to get back down. This led to serious congestion and sometimes even dangerous pile-ups. So it was decided to break through the uppermost floor of the back annexe to the flat roof of the landing. This created a direct connection with the attic of the front house, and visitors could follow a one-way traffic pattern through the building. There was still no admission charge at this time, but visitors were asked to make a voluntary contribution. In addition, the Stichting received a subsidy from the Dutch government for educational activities aimed at awakening the public conscience to current forms of discrimination and intolerance.

The finances needed for the restoration formed a new problem, but by means of another collection appeal the necessary amount was raised. At the end of 1970 the Anne Frank House closed for a few months for restoration. A new exhibition was set up at the same time dealing with the history of Nazi Germany and the persecution of the Jews. A number of exhibit panels were devoted to 'current centres of discrimination and persecution'.

More visitors and activities

In 1971 the Anne Frank House was reopened with great festivity. The restoration and redesign of the building made clear that it was no longer wise to keep the necessary maintenance dependent on gifts. Beginning with that year, an admission fee was charged.

The interest from home and abroad continued to grow. This was apparent not only in the number of visitors but also through the activities developed by the Stichting. In temporary exhibitions, discussion sessions and courses, attention was devoted to such themes as human rights, apartheid in South Africa or the Vietnam war. In 1974 an international conference was organized entitled 'Migrants in Europe'. Among the

In one of the rooms in the front house, around 1965: newspaper clippings and diary editions on display.

1971: the new exhibition about the Second World War and the persecution of the Jews.

One of the young people's congresses from the sixties.
Left, Otto Frank, who was usually present.

important exhibitions were '2000 Years of anti-Semitism' and 'Ultra-Right in Western Europe'. In 1978 the number of visitors had risen to 294,833. In 1979 in the 'diary attic', the attic of the front house of 263 Prinsengracht, a new permanent exhibition was set up which showed the history of Anne and her family placed in the framework of the rise and fall of Nazi Germany. Photographs never before published gave visitors a penetrating view of Anne's life story. For this exhibition, Mr Frank made available original documents and Anne's manuscripts.

In 1980 the entrance was changed. Up until then, entrance tickets had been sold on the second floor at the top of the long stairway. The row of waiting visitors made for a cramped and unsafe situation. This ended with the moving of the admission desk to the ground floor. From then on, the public entered the house through the broad doors of the former warehouse.

The growing number of visitors made for more changes during the following years. The elaborate exhibition at the beginning of the museum route was replaced by a short introductory video. In a few minutes, this provided a picture of Anne's life story and the story of the Secret Annexe. Reconstructions of the furnished hiding place which were recorded for this purpose were able to explain a great deal. In the Annexe itself a passageway was cut through Peter's room to facilitate traffic flow. The exhibit in the front attic was not changed during the eighties, but since 1988 Anne's first diary, on permanent loan from the Netherlands State Institute for War Documentation, has been added to it. A small display on the second floor considers national socialism, anti-Semitism and the occupation of the Netherlands from 1940-45. A permanent slide show is also found there. A number of temporary exhibitions from that period dealt with racism in the Netherlands (for example, 'Black-White '84') and with current developments concerning neo-fascism in Western Europe. In 1989 attention was again given to anti-Semitism, but on a broader basis and with more pictorial material. Nobel Prize winner Elie Wiesel opened this exhibition. Anticipating future adaptations in the

Children in thé Annexe during a tour.

The permanent exhibition in the attic of the front house, at the end of the eighties.

Exhibition on the Netherlands and the Second World War on the second floor of the museum.

Floor plan, 263 Prinsengracht, former layout

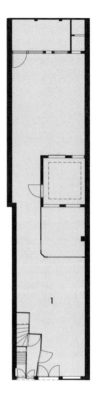 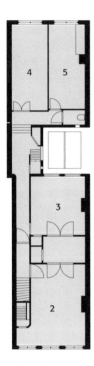 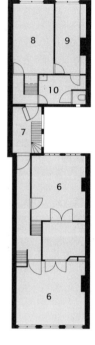 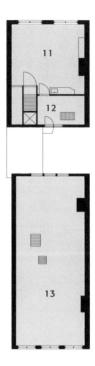

A. ground flood

1. warehouse

B. first floor

2. front office
3. Kugler and Kleiman's office
4. Otto Frank's private office
5. office kitchen

C. second floor

6. spice storage area
7. landing with bookcase
8. Frank family's room
9. Anne's room
10. washing room with toilet

D. third floor

11. Van Daan family's room
12. Peter van Daan's room
13. attic

Floor plan, 263 Prinsengracht, current layout

From canalside house to museum

A. ground flood

1. entrance
2. reception area

B. first floor

3. exhibition hall
4. Otto Frank's private office
5. office kitchen

C. second floor

6. introduction room
7. landing with bookcase
8. Frank family's room
9. Anne's room
10. washing room with toilet
11. exhibition room

D. third floor

12. Van Daan family's room
13. Peter van Daan's room
14. landing to the front house
15. exhibition loft

museum, a number of renovations were made in 1991 in the front sections of 263 and 265 Prinsengracht. On the first floor of the front house at no. 263, where the museum shop had been located, a room for temporary exhibitions was created. The completely refurbished museum shop was moved to the large room near the exit.

The year 1992

The activities of the Anne Frank Stichting have grown considerably in the course of the years. The house on the Prinsengracht is more than a monument to a tragic past, and maintaining it is an important responsibility. Both through the museum and through its educational and informational activities, the Anne Frank Stichting provides a link from the past to the present. Expressions of anti-Semitism, discrimination and racism are still the order of the day, both in the Netherlands and abroad.

In the museum, changing exhibitions draw attention to such subjects as growing intolerance against minorities, politically organized racism or aggression against refugees. Interest in the Anne Frank House continues to grow: in 1990 the number of visitors rose above 600,000 for the first time.

The specialized library holds a large collection of books, magazines, newspaper and magazine articles and audiovisual material from the Netherlands and abroad. Part of the collection concerns present-day subjects such as expressions of anti-Semitism, racism and discrimination. The collection also concentrates on the Second World War. Finally, the 'Anne Frank Collection' contains unique photos, books, clippings and other materials which relate to Anne Frank, her family and the others who went into hiding in the Secret Annexe.

The educational department develops programmes in the museum, gives courses and produces material which can be used in schools and other settings. The annual Anne Frank Kranten (Anne Frank Newspapers) attract international interest as well. In 1985 the exhibition 'De Wereld van Anne Frank' ('Anne Frank in the World') was

'Holland ~~white~~ for everybody', a picture from one of the exhibitions on racism today.

The Annexe amidst the surrounding buildings.

The museum shop, 1992.

developed which gives a picture of developments between 1929 and 1945. This travelling exhibition was issued in various languages and has been seen in North and South America, various Eastern and Western European countries and Japan.

To carry on with all these activities, the Stichting relies in the first place on financial support from both the Netherlands and abroad. A small part of the work is financed through subsidies from the Dutch government, incidental subsidies for projects and from the sale of the Stichting's own products and services. For the preponderance of its activities the Stichting is dependent on income from the museum and voluntary contributions from funds, businesses and individual visitors.

A glimpse into the future

The Stichting's number of employees has kept pace with the expansion of its activities. In 1992 the Anne Frank Stichting staff numbers more than eighty. Their work takes place in three buildings, all situated around the inner garden behind the Anne Frank House.

The space for visitors in the museum, however, has remained the same for years. Congestion occurs regularly, by which visitors are hardly in a condition to experience the sense of imprisonment in the back annexe or to view the exhibitions quietly. On busy days the museum has to close its doors from time to time. The Anne Frank Stichting has been looking for a solution to this acute space shortage for several years.

In 1990 the City of Amsterdam granted permission to expand the museum beyond the current buildings to the plot on the corner of the Prinsengracht and the Westermarkt. This new building will accommodate the offices. By expanding the space, a visit to the museum can be spread over a larger surface area. Service to visitors will significantly improve. In addition to a large hall for temporary exhibitions, the new building will house a film hall, media library and museum shop. Fewer and fewer visitors to the Anne Frank House went through the war years themselves. This affects

'Refugees and Europe': a present-day exhibition in the summer of 1991.

1929-1945 | APRIL 18TH– MAY 16TH | ANNE FRANK IN THE WORLD

The travelling exhibition 'Anne Frank in the World' in East London, April 1987: the entrance is smeared with anti-Semitic slogans.

The travelling exhibition at the European Parliament, Strasbourg, June 1990.

the information which is provided in the museum and the manner of presentation. The buildings at 263 and 265 Prinsengracht will be completely devoted to exhibition space. The Secret Annexe itself will be restored wherever necessary and, it goes without saying, will be kept in its original state.

Brief Reference List

Anne Frank, *The diary of a young girl*, London/New York 1989.
Anne Frank, *Tales from the secret annexe*, Middlesex 1986.
Anne Frank Stichting, *Anne Frank in the world 1929 - 1945*, Amsterdam 1992.
Miep Gies, *Anne Frank remembered*, London/New York 1987.
The Netherlands State Institute for War Documentation, *The diary of Anne Frank; the critical edition*, London/New York 1989.
Willy Lindwer, *The last seven months*, New York 1991.

With thanks to:

Anne Frank Fonds / Basel
Miep and Jan Gies

Photo credits

(numbers refer to pages, (t) = top, (b) = bottom.)
ABC: 61
Benthem/Crouwel Architekten: 91(b)
Hans Boerrigter: 91(t), 95
Jan-Erik Dubbelman: 93(b)
David Hoffman: 93(t)
Wubbo de Jong: 52
KLM Aerocarto: 5, 9
Madeleen Ladee: 92
Martijn Luns: 87
Nationaal Fotopersbureau: 73
Rijksinstituut voor Oorlogsdocumentatie:
    12, 13, 19, 22, 23(t), 26, 31, 48, 49, 53(t), 56, 57(b), 58, 59, 74
Maria Austria / Stichting Particam:
    21, 25(t), 32, 33(b), 34(b), 35(b), 37,
    38, 40, 41, 76, 77, 79, 81
Spaarnestad: 70
Maarten van de Velde: 34(t), 54, 82, 83
Egbert van Zon: 84, 85
Remaining illustrations:
    ©Anne Frank Fonds, Basel and/or Anne Frank Stichting, Amsterdam

Colofon

© *All texts of Anne Frank:*
    Anne Frank Fonds, Basel

Translation: Nancy Forest-Flier
Design: ontwerpbureau Amsterdam
    Martijn Luns / Peter Vermeulen bNO
Printing: Boom Ruygrok Offset bv / Haarlem

© Anne Frank Stichting, Amsterdam 1992

ISBN 90 12 06601 8